THE INFINITY

OF INTIMACY

THE INFINITY
OF INTIMACY

FROM BIOLOGICAL FAMILY TO
EVOLUTIONARY FAMILY

. . .

Awakening to the Intimate Universe

One Mountain, Many Paths: Oral Essays

Volume Nineteen

DR. MARC GAFNI AND
BARBARA MARX HUBBARD

Authors: Marc Gafni and Barbara Marx Hubbard
Title: The Infinity of Intimacy
Identifiers: ISBN 979-8-88834-026-4 (electronic)
ISBN 979-8–88834–025–7 (paperback)

© 2025 Marc Gafni

Edited by Talya Bloom, Rachel Keune, and Elena Maslova-Levin

World Philosophy and Religion Press,
St. Johnsbury, VT

in conjunction with

IP Integral Publishers

https://worldphilosophyandreligion.org

CONTENTS

CHAPTER 5   OUR CRISIS IS A BIRTH: ALL CRISIS IS A CRISIS OF INTIMACY

CHAPTER 6   ENLIGHTENMENT IS INTIMACY WITH ALL PEOPLE AND ALL THINGS

CHAPTER 7   MY CRISIS IS MY BIRTH—REALITY DESIRES MY BIRTH

CHAPTER 8   INCLUDING AND TRANSCENDING: FROM BIOLOGICAL FAMILY TO EVOLUTIONARY FAMILY

CHAPTER 9   INCLUDING AND TRANSCENDING: FROM BIOLOGICAL FAMILY TO SOUL ROOT EVOLUTIONARY FAMILY, PART 2

CHAPTER 10 THE BLESSING OF THE FATHER: THE PERSONAL, THE POLITICAL, THE COSMIC

CHAPTER 11 THE INTIMACY CRISIS: WHY THE ATLANTIC MAGAZINE GOT IT WRONG

EDITORIAL NOTE ABOUT AUTHORSHIP, EDITING, AND THE RADICAL CONTEXT FOR THIS SERIES

ORAL ESSAYS FROM THE ONE MOUNTAIN, MANY PATHS WEEKLY BROADCAST

This volume is part of the Oral Essays library, a series of lightly edited, compiled transcripts of oral teachings given by Dr. Marc Gafni and the late Barbara Marx Hubbard in their weekly online broadcast, *One Mountain, Many Paths,* which they co-founded in 2017. Originally called an "Evolutionary Church," *One Mountain, Many Paths* became a key venue for the articulation of an inspired and deeply grounded new Story of Value in response to the meta-crisis. Marc and Barbara—together with Zak Stein,[1] Kristina Kincaid, Ken Wilber, Sally Kempton, Lori Galperin, Aubrey Marcus and dozens of other thought-leaders over the years—began to articulate what they call a World Philosophy and World Religion[2] as a context for our diversity.

---

1   Zak, together with Ken Wilber, has been Marc's primary intellectual partner and an initiate lineage holder in CosmoErotic Humanism.

2   This project is grounded in four core organizational frameworks: 1) The Center for World Philosophy and Religion, co-founded by Marc Gafni, Zachary Stein, Sally Kempton, and Ken Wilber, and chaired over the years by John P. Mackey, Barbara Marx Hubbard, Aubrey Marcus, Gabrielle Anwar and Shareef Malnik, Carrie Kish and Adam Bellow, and Kathleen J. Brownback. 2) The Office for the Future, chaired by Stephanie Valcke and Ivan Bossyut. 3) The World Philosophy and Religion Press, founded and chaired by Aubrey Marcus, together with Marc Gafni and Zachary Stein. 4) The Foundation for Conscious Evolution, founded by Barbara Marx Hubbard and currently chaired by Peter Fiekowsky. For a complete list of key leadership, see the Office for the Future website, www.officeforthefuture.com.

Until Barbara's passing in 2019, she and Marc transmitted teachings together as evolutionary partners and "whole mates," weaving together insights and transmissions from their decades of practice, study, teaching, and activism into a synergy of wisdom, a grounded vision for future policy across all sectors of society.

Much of the *dharma* material below comes directly from Marc, so it was originally all in quotation marks—but that looked a little odd. So per his suggestion we removed them, and the reader should consider the paragraphs on the next several pages as one extended quote from him. We are joyfully grateful to Marc for the clarity of his *dharma*, the elegance and "second simplicity" of this language, and the mad, Outrageous Love with which he transmits his teachings.

Barbara and Marc called the mission of *One Mountain* "a Planetary Awakening in Evolutionary Love Through Unique Self Symphonies." We are an evolutionary community with a deeply grounded, radically alive, and "post-tragic" revolutionary spirit. We are activating a new humanity and awakening as a new species: *Homo amor*, the fulfillment of *Homo sapiens*.

One Mountain is committed to articulating a Story of Value that can become the ground for the new society that must be birthed in response to the meta-crisis. We recognize that we are living at a pivotal moment in history. In this "time between stories," the great moral imperative is to tell the new Story of Value. It is ours to do, personally and collectively, with great trembling and ecstatic joy.

FROM DOGMA TO DHARMA: ETERNAL AND EVOLVING FIRST PRINCIPLES AND FIRST VALUES

The teachings are grounded in decades of deep study across many wisdom traditions. Over the years, week by week, these teachings were incrementally developed within the framework of the *One Mountain, Many Paths* broadcast. We often refer to these teachings as *dharma*.

This word was originally used in lineage traditions to refer to something like universal law. This is a crucial realization: just as there is universal law in mathematical value, there is also a sense of universal law in ethics and value.

Historically, *dharma* often devolved into unchanging dogma. Evolution was ignored, and the natural process of *dharma* evolution became disconnected from its deep, eternal context. The weakness of the word *dharma* is that too often it did not include the evolving insights of the sciences, it confused local cultural truths with universal truths, and it used words like "eternal," as in "eternal Tao," as opposed to words like "evolution."

Eternal came to mean unchanging, and that kind of thinking often led to overly ethnocentric readings of *dharma*. Local systems would claim their religious and cultural insights as immutable, which stood in the way of the emergence of a genuine world Story of Value that is real, inherent to Cosmos, and backed by the Universe—even as it is also always evolving.

Or, as we often say, "eternal value is evolving value. The eternal Tao is the evolving Tao."

We have shown that, emergent from profound insights in the "interior sciences," eternal does not mean unchanging in time; it means what we call the deeper Field of ErosValue that is beneath culture, geography, and history, which lives beneath all individual and collective values, and beneath time and space itself.

As such, we have gradually transitioned from the term *dharma* to the term *Value*, in the sense of the Field of Value that lives beneath all values. This Field of Value discloses as First Principles and First Values embedded in a Story of Value.

Indeed, as the interior sciences knew and the exterior sciences imply, Reality arises in a Field of ErosValue in which an entire set of mathematical, musical, molecular, moral, and mystical values are the very ground of all being. That Field of Value is eternal—the true ground of the Good, True and Beautiful—even as it is evolving.

But of course, it is equally critical not just to talk about evolving value, but to ground the evolving value in its true nature, the eternal Field of First Principles and First Values, always reaching for ever more life, ever more love, ever more care, ever more depth, ever more uniqueness, ever more intimate communion, and ever more transformation.

As such, when we refer to the word *dharma*, which still appears in these texts together with the word value, we refer to an evolving *dharma* grounded in an *eternal and evolving* Field of Value. Indeed, eternity and evolution are two faces of the whole, opposites joined at the hip, that characterize the nature of our Cosmos in virtually all of its expressions.

It's in these terms that we ground a robust world philosophy that integrates the validated, leading-edge insights of premodern traditional wisdom, modern wisdom, and more recent postmodern insights, weaving them together into a new whole greater than the sum of its parts.

This new whole is a shared Story of Value rooted in First Principles and First Values that are both eternal and evolving.

These First Principles and First Values of Cosmos are woven together into a new Story of Value as a context for our diversity, a new Universe Story. This new story gives us the best possible responses we have to the mystery, and to the great questions:

- Who am I? Who are we?
- Where am I? Where are we?
- What should I do? What should we do?

It is only through such a shared Universe Story—a narrative of identity and ethos as a context for our blessed diversity—that we can realize how what unites us is so much greater than what divides us.

Only a new Story of Value will allow us to both respond to the meta-crisis and participate together in birthing the most true, good, and beautiful world that we already know is possible.

THIS ORAL ESSAYS SERIES IS AN ENTRYWAY TO THE GREAT LIBRARY OF COSMOEROTIC HUMANISM

This Oral Essays series is part of the overarching project of the Great Library at the Center for World Philosophy and Religion, led by Dr. Marc Gafni, together with Dr. Zak Stein. The aim of the Great Library project is to articulate a robust and comprehensive new Story of Value, CosmoErotic Humanism, in the form of dozens of well-researched and extensively footnoted academic works.

Our vision is to provide the philosophical framework that will be vital for navigating humanity through this time of immense crisis and transformation.

To begin your journey into CosmoErotic Humanism, we tenderly refer you to the book *First Principles and First Values*, co-authored by Marc Gafni, Zak Stein, and Ken Wilber, under the name David J. Temple. David J. Temple is a pseudonym created for enabling ongoing collaborative authorship at the Center for World Philosophy and Religion. The two primary authors behind David J. Temple are Marc Gafni and Zak Stein, and for different projects, specific writers will be named as part of the collaboration, such as Ken Wilber and others.

Three other volumes complete this introduction: *A Return to Eros*, by Marc Gafni and Kristina Kincaid; *Your Unique Self*, by Marc Gafni; and *Education in a Time between Worlds*, by Zak Stein.

We hope that the Oral Essays in the present volume, with their informal style of transmission, will serve as an allurement and entryway for you into the more formal books of the Great Library that provide the robust intellectual underpinnings of the new Story of Value.

A NOTE ABOUT THE EDITORS

This Oral Essays collection has been edited by students of the new story of CosmoErotic Humanism. Each of us has actively participated in *One Mountain, Many Paths*, and most of us have been in deep "Holy of Holies" study with Dr. Marc Gafni for many years.

We have been privileged to find ourselves well-versed in the teachings, and even emerging as lineage-holders of CosmoErotic Humanism.[3]

We view this editing project as a privilege and a deep practice of study and clarification. We experience ourselves as a *mystical editing society*, frequently meeting and conversing together about the content—the depth of knowledge and wisdom offered here—as well as the technical intricacies involved with publishing a beautiful and coherent series of books. In so

---

3 CosmoErotic Humanism is a world philosophical movement aimed at reconstructing the collapse of value at the core of global culture. Much like Romanticism or Existentialism, CosmoErotic Humanism is not merely a theory but a movement that changes the very mood of Reality. It is an invitation to participate in evolving the source code of consciousness and culture towards a cosmocentric *ethos* for a planetary civilization.

The term CosmoErotic Humanism, initially coined by Dr. Gafni and colleagues, points to a complex, multi-faceted, layered, and nuanced evolutionary set of insights that has evolved over decades of intensive research, teaching, and spiritual practice from deep within a wide range of wisdom traditions (including the Wisdom of Solomon lineage tradition, Bodhisattva Buddhism, and Kashmir Shaivism), as well as multiple disciplines including complexity theory, chaos theory, emergence theory, molecular biology, and the more classical disciplines of the humanities.

The seeds of CosmoErotic Humanism were planted with Dr. Marc Gafni's work on a two-volume, 1,000-page opus called *Radical Kabbalah* (Integral Publishers, 2012). This scholarly work, sourced from deep study within the esoteric lineage texts of the Wisdom of Solomon, points to a non-dual, or acosmic, realization which—unlike the prevailing conceptualization of non-duality—does not efface the human being; rather, it is highly humanistic in its nature. The next step in the evolution of CosmoErotic Humanism was the insight that all of Reality is evolving Eros, which lives in, as, and through the human being.

A failure of Eros leads inexorably to the creation of narratives of "pseudo-eros." CosmoErotic Humanism is a response to the modern mental and social breakdown sourced in the proliferation of multiple forms of pseudo-eros and its broken narratives, such as rivalrous conflict governed by win/lose metrics and the dogmatic denial of intrinsic value in Cosmos, which together generate our current "global intimacy disorder."

doing, we function as a "Unique Self Symphony," which itself is a *dharmic* term that connotes an omni-considerate collaboration between realized Unique Selves synergizing our unique gifts into a new emergence greater than the sum of the parts. Even as we worked diligently to standardize our editing styles, meeting on a weekly basis to debate the nuances of phrasing, we also operated from within a deep appreciation of the unique style that each editor brought to his or her work. As such, the reader might notice some variation in editing style among the books.

Please note that Dr. Marc Gafni has not reviewed these edited Oral Essays, as he is deeply engaged in writing the formal books of the Great Library. But he has been generous in responding to questions and providing overall guidance in the project. Overall, as Marc's students and students of the *dharma*, we have made it a key project at the Center to publish these pieces of work relatively independently.

OUR UNIQUE ORAL-ESSAY EDITING STYLE PRESERVES THE ENERGY OF THE ORIGINAL TRANSMISSION

Dr. Marc Gafni is a uniquely gifted teacher whose oral transmission is imbued with a quality that has proven transformative for his students. Many of us feel mystically transformed by both the content and the underlying energy of the transmission style. Therefore, as we like to say, *trust the magic ways the dharma comes through your unique understanding!*

As Marc's empowered students, colleagues, and beloved friends, we have a deep knowing that these teachings are vital for the survival and thriving of humanity as we know it, and we recognize the importance of publishing his teachings in a written format that will be accessible by future generations. At the same time, we sought to preserve the Eros of the original oral transmission with all of its nuance, power, and depth. Our intention in the editing process, to the greatest extent possible, has been to keep these spoken artifacts intact in order to maintain the flow of the original transmission. We have therefore chosen not to engage in intensive formal editing, as we found that doing so resulted in the loss of the energetic transmission that is so key to fully receiving the *dharma*.

After experimenting with many ways to present these texts, we developed a specific way of laying out the text on the page. Marc, in collaboration with Zak Stein and Russian intellectual/artist Elena Maslova-Levin—and ultimately all of the editors, through many conversations—developed a unique, artistic presentation of the text, using bolding, italics, bullet points, and other stylistic features which together serve to accentuate the immediacy of the oral transmission.

As part of this editing style, intended to preserve the integrity of the original transmission, we have refrained from removing the frequent recapitulations of key themes. We found that each recapitulation contributes something vital to the rhythm and music beneath the words, like the beating drum of our hearts. These recapitulations not only review previous material but also add important new emphases, perspectives, and elements of the new Story of Value. We ask for your patience as a reader to trust the rhythm of these texts, and we trust you as a reader to have the depth and steadiness to find your way through.

KEY COMPONENTS: LINK TO THE ORIGINAL BROADCAST, EVOLUTIONARY LOVE CODES AND PRAYER

To supplement the written word, each episode includes a QR code linking to the original broadcast on YouTube, as well as occasional links to featured songs and video clips.

Each episode also centers around an "Evolutionary Love Code," formulated by Marc. These codes are part of the ongoing articulation and distillation of the *dharma* as it unfolds and emerges, week by week, over the course of many years, through the mystical process we call Outrageous Love or Evolutionary Love.

Another core component of the *One Mountain, Many Paths* episodes is what Marc and Barbara called "Evolutionary Prayer." Prayer is experienced in *One Mountain* not in the old fundamentalist sense of a "cosmic vending-machine god" who is alienated from Cosmos. Marc refers to this as the "god you do not and should not believe in"—and he often adds, "the god you don't believe in does not exist."

GOD IS THE INFINITE INTIMATE

In fact, in the *dharma* of CosmoErotic Humanism, a new name for God has emerged: the "Infinite Intimate," who appears in first-, second-, and third-person expressions. Marc first shared this name as he heard it whispered in 2023, although earlier intimations and formulations of the name appeared as early as 2010.

In first person, God is infinitely alive and as intimate as our own first-person experience.

In second person, God is the infinitely intimate Personhood of Cosmos that knows our name and holds us—the God about whom we say, *whenever we fall, we fall into Her hands.* This is the God who is our Beloved, Father, Mother, Lover, and Evolutionary Partner.

Finally, in third person, God inheres in all of the First Principles and First Values of Cosmos, and in the laws of science (both interior and exterior) that govern manifest Reality.

Therefore, we have a realization of God as not only the Infinity of Power but also the Infinity of Intimacy.

In *One Mountain, Many Paths*, we are reclaiming prayer at a higher level of consciousness. And we are reclaiming prayer as deep, alive, loving, and intimate conversations with God as the Infinite Intimate who knows our name.

REFLECTING ON THE CO-CREATION BETWEEN DR. MARC GAFNI AND BARBARA MARX HUBBARD

Barbara and Marc met five years before Barbara passed. As Barbara said so often, "before I met Marc, I was sure that I was done." Barbara had taught so beautifully for decades, focusing particularly on a powerful articulation of "conscious evolution."

Indeed, it would not be inaccurate to say that Barbara was the greatest storyteller of conscious evolution of her time.

Conscious evolution was also a premise in Marc's thinking, but drawn from an entirely different set of sources and experiences. Barbara drew from the classical sources of evolutionary spirituality, such as Teilhard de Chardin, Buckminster Fuller, and many others.

Indeed, she was closely associated with Fuller, and was perhaps de Chardin's most ardent intellectual devotee.

Marc drew a somewhat different vision of conscious evolution from the interior sciences of the great wisdom traditions, with a primary emphasis on what he refers to as the "Solomon lineages," merged together with careful readings of the leading edges of the sciences.

In the old version of conscious evolution, the movement from unconscious to conscious was a movement of evolution by chance to evolution by choice.

Together Marc and Barbara evolved the old version of conscious evolution, pointing out that evolution itself was always in some sense conscious, but as Marc formulated it, the awakening to conscious evolution refers to the awakening of evolution as human consciousness, coupled with the human realization of being conscious evolution in person, and the human capacity to locate oneself within the context of the larger evolutionary story.

Marc focused his attention on an entirely different dimension of Reality, which he and his colleagues began to call CosmoErotic Humanism. The Intimate Universe, Homo amor, Unique Self and Unique Self Symphonies,

God as the Infinity of Intimacy, Eros and the CosmoErotic Universe, distinctions like Role Mate, Soul Mate and Whole Mate, the Four Selves, Evolutionary Love, Outrageous Love, Evolution: the Love Story of the Universe, First Principles and First Values, Evolving Perennialism, the Evolution of Love, and many more are terms articulated by Gafni and shared with Barbara in their conversation, study, and creative engagement.

Some terms they coined together, for example "a Planetary Awakening in Love through Unique Self Symphonies", where Gafni described Unique Self Symphonies, and Barbara aligned her vision of a planetary Pentecost to Marc's vision of Unique Self Symphonies.

Other key terms were unique and articulated by Barbara, for example: conscious evolution, teleros, telerotic, from joining genes to joining genius, regenopause, vocational arousal, birthing of humanity, synergy engine, and of course her work around what she called the Wheel of Co-creation.

Ultimately, Marc and Barbara attempted to synergize their work in what they called the Wheel of Co-creation 2.0. Barbara and Marc experienced themselves as merging their respective *dharma* into what they began to refer to as Conscious Evolution 2.0, or later, CosmoErotic Humanism.

The first 129 episodes of One Mountain, Many Paths took place in the last period of Barbara's life and reflect the depth and texture of the stunning evolutionary whole-mate meeting between her and Marc.

As Barbara was deep in study with Marc, a lot of what she shared in Evolutionary Church was the *dharma* of their deep study and collaboration. Although sometimes it may be clear who is speaking, we generally publish these early episodes in what we are calling "one voice."

The first 129 episodes, with Marc and Barbara together, have been grouped chronologically. Episodes 130 to 400 and onwards, which were transmitted by Marc, have been grouped by topic.

THE INVITATION

We invite you to find your way into this revolution. Each one of our Unique Selves and unique gifts are desperately needed as we co-create this new Story of Value together, as part of the covenant between generations, for the sake of the whole.

Let's *play a larger game* and evolve the very source code of consciousness and culture together.

With mad love,

The Editors

LOVE OR DIE

LOCATING OURSELVES: ARTICULATING THE ESSENTIAL CONTEXT FOR THE ONE MOUNTAIN, MANY PATHS ORAL ESSAYS

SETTING OUR INTENTION

Intention setting is everything.

We're here—as da Vinci was with his cohort in the Renaissance—**to play a larger game, to participate in the evolution of love, which is to tell the new Story of Value rooted in First Principles and First Values.**

- Our intention is to recognize the critical historical juncture in which we find ourselves.
- Our intention is to take our seat at the table of history and to say, *we take responsibility for this.*
- Our intention is to participate as revolutionaries for the sake of the whole.

What we're here to do is revolution; revolution for the sake of the evolution of love.

It's a revolution for the sake of the trillions of unborn lives that will not manifest:

- The unborn loves
- The unborn creativity
- The unborn goodness
- The unborn truth
- The unborn beauty

All of it looks to us.

Not because we're engaged in grandiosity. Not at all!

- We're trembling before She.
- We're trembling with joy at the privilege.
- We're trembling with joy at the responsibility.
- We're trembling with joy at the Possibility of Possibility.
- We have to enact a new story in this moment of time. Because it is only a new story that can change the vector of history.

The most revolutionary act that we can do—the greatest moral imperative of this time—**is to articulate a new story at this time between worlds and this time between stories**.

Story is not made up, as postmodernity suggests. **We all live in inescapable frameworks; our framework is the story we live in.** Right now, Reality lives according to win/lose metrics, a story that is generating existential risk. **We need to change that story.**

When we change that story, when we tell a new story—not a made-up story, but a new Story of Value, rooted in First Principles and First Values—**then it all changes.**

We need to participate in the evolution of the source code of consciousness and culture, which is the evolution of love.

It's the most important, exciting, evolutionary, revolutionary act that we can do to alleviate suffering: to be lovers.

Like Rumi, the great poet of Sufism, we have to be "mad lovers," because it's the only sanity.

To be mad lovers is to see around the corner, to not be so obsessed with the details of the contractions of my life.

Let me see bigger.

Let me take complete care of myself in every possible way, let me completely attend to those in my circle of intimacy and influence, and then—*let me expand my circle.*

That's what we're here for.

- ◆ Our intention is to participate in the *LoveForce*, the *LoveIntelligence*, the *LoveBeauty*, the *LoveDesire* that literally animates Cosmos all the way up and all the way down.
- ◆ Our intention is to participate in the evolution of love.

[*In the next few pages we will cover some key concepts which are essential to locating ourselves and setting the context for all the One Mountain, Many Paths Oral Essays. —Eds.*]

OVERVIEW: EROS IS NO LONGER A LUXURY—IT'S LOVE OR DIE

Eros is life.

The failure of Eros destroys life.

Our lack of Eros is poised to destroy the world.

All civilizations have fallen because the stories that they lived in were, in some sense, stories based on rivalrous conflict governed by win/lose metrics. Every civilization was weakened by interior polarization caused by the lack of a shared Story of Value.

We now have a global civilization, but we haven't created a shared Story of Value.

We haven't solved the generator functions that caused all civilizations to fall. Our global civilization has exponential technologies and extraction models depleting the Earth of resources that took billions of years to create, which is going to lead to a civilizational collapse.

Existential risk is risk to our very existence.

The choice is clear: love or die.

It's that simple.

Eros is no longer a luxury. It is an absolute necessity for the survival of the individual and the planet.

In the last half a century, modern psychology has documented an age-old truth: a fully nourished baby who is not held in loving arms will die.

So too, our world, both personal and global—even with all the resources of intelligence and technology at our disposal—will die without being held in love, in the embrace of Eros.

We must embrace a personal path of love and a global politics of love.

Not ordinary love. Not love which is "mere human sentiment," but Eros, or what we sometimes call Outrageous Love, which is the heart of existence itself.

We live in a world of outrageous pain.

The only response is Outrageous Love.

WHAT IS EROS?

Eros is the experience of radical aliveness, moving towards, seeking, desiring ever deeper contact and ever greater wholeness.[4] Eros is the core fabric of Reality's being and the motivational architecture of Reality's becoming.

Eros is what animates the evolutionary impulse itself, from the very inception of Cosmos all the way to our very selves, who awaken to the realization that the evolutionary impulse throbs uniquely in each of us.

The realization of human awakening and transformation that lies at the core of the interior sciences is the invitation—or even the urgent and desperate demand—of a madly loving Cosmos animated by infinities of power and infinities of intimacy.

The demand—the desperate invitation, the plea, the tender and fierce command of Cosmos that lives inside every human being—is to awaken: to awaken to our true nature as unique incarnations of Eros and Ethos that are needed and desperately desired by All-That-Is. Said slightly differently: Reality is Eros. Or: God is Eros.

The failure of Eros destroys life. The collapse of Eros is always the hidden (or not so hidden) root cause for the collapse of ethics.

This is true both personally and collectively. We live in a moment of a world-wide and personal collapse of Eros. Our lack of Eros is poised to destroy

---

4 We define Eros through what we refer to as the Eros equation (one of a series of what we call interior science equations):

> *Eros = Radical Aliveness* x *Desiring (Growing + Seeking)* x *Deeper Contact* x *Greater Wholeness* x *Self Actualization/Self Transcendence (Creation [Destruction])*

There are good reasons for the formal language of the interior science equations in these writings, and the reader is invited to explore them on their own, in particular, in our work, David J. Temple, *First Principles and First Values: Forty-Two Propositions on CosmoErotic Humanism, the Meta-Crisis, and the World to Come* (World Philosophy and Religion, 2024).

the world. Humanity is currently experiencing what has come to be known as existential risk, a risk to our very existence, or what I will refer to as the Second Shock of Existence.

EXISTENTIAL RISK: THE SECOND SHOCK OF EXISTENCE

The first shock of existence is the death of the human being—the realization that we will die, which dawns in human consciousness at the beginning of history. We are not talking about the biological fact of death but the *existential* realization of death. Although the interior sciences disclose that death is a portal between two days (there is vast empirical,[5] philosophical,[6] and anthro-ontological evidence[7] for the continuity of consciousness[8]), death is also, in our own direct surface experience, a stark end. And that is obviously not a bug but a feature in the system.

---

5   We refer to evidence gathered by the most serious of researchers, beginning with Henry and Edith Sedgwick at Cambridge University and William James at Harvard University, and continuing in highly rigorous form for the last 150 years, as recapitulated by Whiteheadian scholar David Ray Griffin in multiple volumes. See also, for example, Dean Radin, *Real Magic: Unlocking Your Natural Psychic Abilities to Create Everyday Miracles* (Potter/TenSpeed/Harmony, 2018), *The Conscious Universe: The Scientific Truth of Psychic Phenomena* (HarperCollins, 2010), and other books. Or see the earlier classic by Frederic William Henry Myers, *Human Personality and Its Survival of Bodily Death* (Longmans, Green, 1907).

6   This requires a cogent analysis of materialism and dualism, and the introduction of the far more cogent third possibility which we have called "pan-interiority."

7   We discuss Anthro-Ontology in some depth in *First Principles and First Values*, and see also the fuller conversation in David J. Temple, *First Principles and First Values: Towards an Evolving Perennialism: Introducing the Anthro-Ontological Method*—both published by World Philosophy and Religion Press, in Conjunction with Integral Publishers. For now, we will simply define it as an "innate and clear interior gnosis directly available to the human being."

8   See Dr. Marc Gafni and Dr. Zachary Stein's essay in preparation, "Beyond Death: Anthro-Ontology, Philosophy, and Empiricism." This essay is slated to appear in the book *Towards a World Religion: Homo Amor Essays*. The essay is also the ground for a larger book by the same authors, *Twelve Portals to Life Beyond Death: Responding to the Second Shock of Existence,* in which we discuss three forms of material: the empirical, the philosophical, and the anthro-ontological, and show how each form discredits the notion of death as the end.

Our first-person experience is that death ends this life. It is not the *totality* of our experience if we go deeper inside, but it is obviously intended to be the central, potent, and painful dimension of every human life. Indeed, as Ernest Becker potently reminded us, the denial of death is at our peril.

All the stories and all the plotlines and all the threads of living end at that moment. Whatever happens beyond, we have an actual experience of ending. **Paradoxically, that ending, the experience of the finality of mortality, is what presses us into life.** From the implicit demand of the first shock of existence, human beings were activated and pressed into creative emergence, and what emerged was all of human culture, both interior and exterior.

The second shock of existence is the realization of the potential death of all humanity. After all the stages of human history—matter, life, and mind in all of their stages of evolutionary unfolding—we have come to this place in the evolution of humanity, in which the gap between our exponentially expanding exterior technologies and our stalled (or even regressing) interior technologies of value has created dire catastrophic and existential risks.

This gap generates extraction models and exponential growth curves, rivalrous conflicts based on win/lose metrics, tragedies of the commons, and multipolar traps, in which everyone has to keep producing to the nth degree, including weaponized exponential threats to our very existence because we are afraid that the other parties are going to do it and not be transparent—hide it from us and then dominate us.

GENERATOR FUNCTIONS FOR EXISTENTIAL RISK

Let's outline clearly the main *generator functions for existential risk*.

Rivalrous conflicts governed by zero-sum, win/lose metrics. Rivalrous conflicts generate extraction models at the core of the economic system and exponential growth curves. Both of these drive and are driven by a contrived system of artificially manufactured desires and needs, delivered into culture by ever more precise forms of micro-targeting to individuals and groups through the ever more immersive environment of the internet.

Next, rivalrous conflicts and exponential growth curves animated by win/lose metrics generate **complicated, fragile world systems** highly vulnerable to myriad forms of collapse. Fragile local systems are made exponentially more fragile on a global level by our inability to meet global challenges with social, legal, political, economic, and ethical infrastructures that remain largely local.

All of this is a direct result of the failure to develop more adequate interior technologies that would be sufficiently compelling to displace "rivalrous conflict governed by win/lose metrics" as the motivational architecture for the human life world.

This failure has led to the conditions that will cause the implosion of systems that are already and quite literally on the brink of collapsing themselves. That's what we mean by the *second shock of existence.*

To recapitulate: the second shock of existence is not the death of the human being, but the potential death of humanity.

It is the *Death Star* moment of our species.

THE DECONSTRUCTION OF INTRINSIC VALUE

We stand in this moment poised between utopia and dystopia, at a time between worlds and a time between stories. We need a new Story of Value, eternal yet evolving, rooted in First Principles and First Values, which would become a universal grammar of value and a context for our diversity.

This is exactly what the Renaissance was. It was a time between worlds and a time between stories. In the Renaissance, we had been recently challenged by the Black Death, a pandemic that swept across Europe. The Black Death destroyed between a third to half of Europe and a huge part of

Asia. People died horrifically, brutally, in the streets. They had no idea how to meet this challenge, and so, in response to the Black Death, da Vinci and Ficino and their cohorts understood that they had to tell a new Story of Value.

That story was the story of modernity. Did they get it right?

- They got part of it right, which birthed, to use Jürgen Habermas' phrase, "the dignities of modernity," such as new ways of gathering information and universal human rights.
- But they also deconstructed the source of Value. They lost the basis for the Good, the True, and the Beautiful.

The basis used to be divine revelation: *God told us.* But this claim was owned by religion, and every religion began to overreach and over-claim. The revelation was thus often mediated through cultural categories and wasn't fully accurate.

Modernity threw out revelation, but was unable to establish a new basis for value.

Value was just assumed to be real. As it says in the founding document of the American Revolution: *We hold these truths to be self-evident*—that is, *we don't really have a basis for value; we just take it as a given.*

In other words, modernity took out a loan of social capital from the traditional world. The source of value was never worked out.

And then, gradually, value began to collapse.

- The Universe Story began to collapse.
- The belief that the Good, the True, and the Beautiful are real began to collapse.
- The belief that Love is real began to collapse.

As Bertrand Russell is reported to have said, "I cannot see how to refute the arguments for the subjectivity of ethical values, but I find myself incapable of believing that all that is wrong with wanton cruelty is that I do not like it."

What do you do if you grew up in a world in which value is not real? A world without a source of value, without a Universe Story, without a story of human identity, without a story of desire, without a narrative of power?

In the words of W.B. Yeats, *the center does not hold.*

- You have a collapse at the very center of society, because you no longer have Eros.
- You no longer have a Reality in which value is real, and so you have this lingering sense of emptiness.
- You have a complete collapse at the very center.
- We become *the hollow men and the stuffed men*, gesture without form.

And that's the source of our current existential risk.

THE DEEPER ROOT CAUSE OF THE META-CRISIS: A GLOBAL INTIMACY DISORDER

Above, I have outlined the major generator functions of existential risk. But there is a deeper cause for the existential risk that lurks underneath the rivalrous conflict governed by win/lose metrics and the fragile systems they engender.

And we cannot take the Death Star down without discerning and addressing this. We have already alluded to this root cause above, but at this point we need to make it more explicit so that, from this context, the adequate root response will become clear.

Modernity threw out revelation, but was unable to establish a new basis for value.

This ostensibly surprising statement can be understood in a few simple steps:

1. All of the catastrophic and existential risk challenges we face are global: from climate change to artificial intelligence, pandemics, systems collapse, and exponential arms races.
2. Every global challenge self-evidently requires a global solution.
3. Global solutions can only be implemented with global co-ordination.
4. Global co-ordination is impossible without global coherence.
5. Global coherence is only possible if there is a global resonance between the parts.
6. Global resonance is only possible if we have global intimacy.

ONLY A SHARED STORY OF VALUE CAN GENERATE GLOBAL INTIMACY

Global intimacy—just like intimacy in a couple—is only possible when there is a shared story.

Not just a shared history, but a shared Story of Value.

- It is only a shared global story that can generate a new emergent quality of intimacy: global intimacy.
- A shared Story of Value must be rooted in shared ordinating values, or what we have called evolving First Values and First Principles.
- Intimacy requires a shared grammar of value as a matrix for a shared Story of Value.

The global intimacy disorder is the root cause for existential risk. The global intimacy disorder underlies the core generator functions for existential risk.

The global intimacy disorder is rooted in the failure to experience ourselves in a field of shared intrinsic value. This failure derives from the deconstruction of value.

Indeed, it is wholly accurate to say that **the root cause of the two generator functions of existential risk is the failed story of intrinsic value, or what we might also call the breakdown of Eros.**

1. The first generator function is **the success story**. Our modern success story is rivalrous conflict governed by win/lose metrics, which violates all the terms of the Intimacy Equation: there is no shared identity and no mutuality of recognition, feeling, value or purpose, and instead of *relative* otherness, there is *alienated* otherness. Such a story generates complicated fragile systems with no allurement or intimacy between the parts, systems which optimize for efficiency (as an expression of win/lose metrics) and not for resiliency and life.

2. The second generator function is **the deconstruction of intrinsic value** itself. The deconstruction of value is the sense that human value does not participate in the intrinsic value of the Real, for the Real is dogmatically declared to have no intrinsic value. Thus, there is no shared identity between the interior of the human being and Reality. There is no common participation in a field of shared intrinsic value. Instead of being intimate with value, we are alienated from value. And only intrinsic value can arouse will: political, moral, and social will.

To sum up, without a shared grammar of value there is no global intimacy, and therefore no global coherence, and no global coordination in response to catastrophic and existential risk, which means, put simply, there will be, quite literally, no future.

HEALING THE GLOBAL INTIMACY DISORDER REQUIRES THE EVOLUTION OF INTIMACY

But we are not hopeless. On the contrary, we are filled with great hope. Hope is a memory of the future. That memory of the future *is* the direct hit that takes down the Death Star, the culture of death. **The direct hit must be**—as it has always been in history—**the emergence of a new stage of evolution.**

Crisis is an evolutionary driver, and every crisis is, at its core, a crisis of intimacy: from the oxygen crisis of the single cells dying which generated multicellular life at the dawn of existence, to the existential risk in this very moment.[9]

The direct hit is therefore structurally self-evident: the evolution of intimacy itself.

What is intimacy, as a structure of Cosmos all the way down and all the way up the evolutionary chain? We engage this inquiry in depth in other writings, but for now we will simply adduce what we have called the "Intimacy Equation":

> *Intimacy = shared identity in the context of [relative] otherness x mutuality of recognition x mutuality of pathos x mutuality of value x mutuality of purpose*

Intimacy is about the capacity of parts to generate a *shared identity* while retaining their otherness, or distinct identity. This requires multiple mutualities, including recognition, pathos (or feeling), value, and purpose. The parts must recognize and feel each other, even as they share value and purpose. But all of this must lead to intimate union—and not pathological

---

9 We demonstrate this principle in some depth in the multi-volume series, *The Universe: A Love Story* (forthcoming) (https://worldphilosophyandreligion.org/early-ontologies), *The Intimate Universe: Global Intimacy Disorder as Cause for Global Action Paralysis* (forthcoming), and in other writings of CosmoErotic Humanism.

fusion, where the distinct identity of the parts disappears—like subatomic particles that successfully become an atom, or two people who successfully become a couple.

THE DECONSTRUCTION OF VALUE IS THE DECONSTRUCTION OF INTIMACY

We have identified the global intimacy disorder as the root cause of existential risk. But the underlying ultimate failure of intimacy is the deconstruction of value itself.

The deconstruction of value means that human value does not participate in any sense of intrinsic value of the Real. This is not about individual *values,* but about *the Field of Value* that underlies all of them. **When the human being**—moved, often sincerely or even nobly, by myriad cultural, historical, and psychological confusions—**claims to have stepped out of the Field of Value, then intimacy itself is deconstructed.**

The deconstruction of value is the deconstruction of intimacy.

In the absence of a shared Story of Value, a story that is an authentic expression of Reality's Eros, a story rooted in *pseudo-Eros* takes center stage and becomes the generator function for existential risk. Our modern pseudo-Eros story is *rivalrous conflict governed by win/lose metrics.* Such a story catalyzes in its wake the second generator function of existential risk: *complicated fragile systems with no allurement or intimacy between the parts.* It is in that sense that we have argued that the first generator function for existential risk is the success story.

- The failure of intimacy is precisely the impotent experience that there is no shared identity between the interior of the human being and Reality. **There is no shared identity in the sense of any kind of common participation in a field of shared intrinsic value.**
- **But only a shared Story of Value can arouse the global will**

required to engage catastrophic and existential risk. For it is only global political, moral, and social will—and we can even say *erotic* will—that can generate the most Good, True and Beautiful world that we have always known is possible.

THE EVOLUTION OF LOVE IS THE TELLING OF A NEW STORY

Coupled with the Intimacy Equation is the scientifically grounded realization, in both the exterior and interior sciences, that Reality is a progressive deepening of intimacies, or, said slightly differently:

Reality is Evolution. Evolution is the evolution of intimacy.

- The evolution of intimacy requires—both personally and collectively—a deeper, more accurate discernment of the nature of our universe, ourselves, and our beloveds.
- This new discernment generates a new global Story of Value.
- The new global Story of Value generates an emergent, heretofore unseen global intimacy and heals the global intimacy disorder.

The new Story of Value is the direct hit that takes down the Death Star and replaces it with the hope that invokes the memory of our best future.

Global intimacy facilitates global coherence, which facilitates global coordination, which activates the possibility of our creative and effectively coordinated global responses to the global meta-crisis in its entirety and its specific expressions.

To solve Bertrand Russell's challenge—the apparent argument for the subjectivity of ethical values—**we have to reground value theory in eternal yet evolving First Principles and First Values, and articulate a new Story of Value.**

This is what we call CosmoErotic Humanism.

CosmoErotic Humanism—together with other emergent strands—**needs to become the ground of a world religion as a context for our diversity**. We need religion, even as we need science, to articulate a shared global grammar of value.

As we said at the beginning, our choice is simple: love or die.

- To love means to participate in the evolution of love, which is the evolution of the human Story of Value.
- To love means to evolve and activate a new cultural enlightenment—rooted in a new narrative of identity, a new narrative of value, a new narrative of intimate communion, a new narrative of desire, a new narrative of power—all of which will birth new narratives of economics and politics.
- The evolution of love is the telling of a new story.

The new story that must be told is a love story, for in fact that is the deepest truth of Reality, rooted in the best exterior and interior sciences, that we have at this moment in time:

- Reality is not merely a fact. Reality is a story.
- Reality is not an ordinary story. Reality is a love story.
- Reality is not an ordinary love story. Reality is an Outrageous Love Story.

Story doesn't mean it's *made-up*.

It means doing the hard work of integrating the validated insights of the traditional world, the modern world, and the postmodern world.

This is the intention at the heart of telling the new story of CosmoErotic Humanism.

ABOUT THIS VOLUME

The Infinity of Intimacy explores "Evolution: The Love Story of the Universe," understood as the evolution of intimacy itself. But one example of this evolution of intimacy is the movement from biological family to a deeper, "evolutionary intimacy" that includes but also transcends traditional roles. CosmoErotic Humanism discloses how we move beyond the bonds of biology into a greater "evolutionary family"—a space where irreducible Unique Selves recognize one another as part of a larger, cosmic symphony. It is before your evolutionary family that you are called to confess your greatness and live out and into your "deepest heart's desires." These are not your ordinary or surface desires but your clarified desires, which by their very nature are your deepest heart's desire.

The framework for the conversation is what we calls the New Universe Story of the Intimate Universe. Evolution here is understood not merely as the progression from simplicity to complexity, but as the progressive deepening of intimacies. The intensification of intimacy as it deepens, widens, and becomes more full is itself the journey from *Homo sapiens* to *Homo amor*, the birth of the possible new human and the new humanity. The Intimate Universe is part of a core dimension in our weaving together a new "Story of Value" for global culture, as a response to the meta-crisis.

Crucially, we are each of us "Unique Selves" that transcend and include psychological separate self and mystical "True Self." We then individuate as irreducibly unique incarnations of the Field of ErosValue, which is the Field of True Self. As Unique Selves, we come together as part of dynamic "Unique Self Symphonies," where every individual plays a unique instrument in the grand symphony of Reality's evolution. There is a common musical score that underlies all of the unique instruments in the great symphony of planetary coherence and intimacy. This is the music and mathematics of "Outrageous Love," for music itself is but sung mathematics—and it is always the mathematics of intimacy.

It is in the Field of Outrageous Love where connections transcend time, biology, and limitation. Here we catch a glimpse of the deeper intimacies, personal and collective, that are both possible and necessary for us to realize in order to traverse this dangerous and potent time between worlds and time between stories.

This volume invites readers to honor the powerful allurement of myriad intimacies that arise along life's path. For ever-evolving and more clarified allurement is the core quality that animates and guides Reality, both individually and globally. Allurement exists at all levels of Reality, from atoms to galaxies, and from quarks to culture. The Cosmos, driven by the evolutionary impulse, calls us to form ever deeper intimate relationships that are not merely random accidents but sacred threads in the great lure of becoming, each one essential to human evolution. Intimacy is thus seen and known directly as an inherent and ever-evolving value of the Universe, at the heart of the new story.

Ultimately, the oral essays collected in *The Infinity of Intimacy* offer a radical reimagining of how we define our place in the evolving Cosmos. We directly experience our identity as unique and celebrated participants in what Marc and Barbara call a "Planetary Awakening in Evolutionary Love Through Unique Self Symphonies." It is a sober yet ecstatic invitation to fully live in the wonder of your Unique Self, in mad, clarified devotion to the larger story of the Creative Cosmos, grounded in eternal and evolving First Principles and First Values. Through all of our explorations we are led back home to the inevitable realization that answers the great question of why we are here, why we exist at all: We are here because *infinity longs for intimacy*—with all of us, and with every single one of us.

Volume 19

These oral essays are lightly edited talks delivered by Marc Gafni and Barbara Marx Hubbard between August 2019 and March 2024.

CHAPTER ONE

CO-CREATING A SYNERGISTIC DEMOCRACY: SYNERGY IS THE NEW INTIMACY OF COSMOS

Episode 151 — August 31, 2019

GLOBAL COMMUNION TOWARDS A PRAGMATIC POLITICS OF LOVE

There's a new quality of time. There's a new invitation to respond in this moment, as we stand poised between utopia—the ability to create a heaven on earth, unlike anything we've ever seen—and dystopia—a deconstruction or a failure of coherence, unlike anything we've ever seen. We can create a world in which we understand that what unites us is so much greater than what divides us.

Our intention that we're setting is to move towards coherence, towards what my friend, Ervin Laszlo—who I just spent an awesome week with in Italy—calls super coherence, or what we call the Intimate Universe: a world that works for everyone.

We want to move towards a world that works for everyone.

It's a world in which we understand that what unites us is so much greater than that which divides us.

It's a world in which **we understand that each of us is the Infinity of Possibility**, and that when we come together and join genius, we are the Possibility of Possibility. We come together to co-create, and we emerge together in this global communion towards a pragmatic politics of Love, where we're reclaiming Love as religion. But not ordinary love—we're reclaiming Outrageous Love.

We're reclaiming Outrageous Love by accessing the inherent feeling of the Universe itself. We know, based on the interior sciences of realization, that the Universe feels, and that the Universe feels Love.

Can you feel it in you? That's where it lives; *the mysteries are within us.* Find inside yourself that place where you feel drawn towards, where you feel allured, where you feel open. That is the Love of Reality flowing in you, as you, and through you. When we come together, and as we develop as Unique Selves—unique expressions of LoveIntelligence and LoveBeauty— we form a Unique Self Symphony.

We are a Unique Self Symphony whose intention is to articulate a politics of Evolutionary Love, to move towards the enactment of a pragmatic politics of Love.

THE HOLY IMPULSE OF THE TRANSGENDER MOVEMENT

The transgender movement is asking all the right questions. There's a political, spiritual, and social impulse in the transgender movement that's on the right track. My colleague, Jordan Peterson, who has very roundly critiqued the transgender movement based on some valid points, misses this core holy impulse. In general, he misses the holy impulse of postmodernity. He sees the weaknesses of postmodernity that we've been pointing out in Integral Theory, CosmoErotic Humanism, and Unique Self Theory for decades now. But he doesn't see the holiness.

The transgender movement is saying something unbelievably important. It's saying that:

Beneath boy/girl, there's something more. I'm more than boy/girl.

That's absolutely right. That's a sacred impulse: *I am more than boy, and I am more than girl.* The problem is when the only remaining identity I have is boy or girl.

- I don't have a national identity.
- I'm no longer white, Jewish, Lutheran, American, French, or Ugandan.
- I don't have a local identity.
- I don't have a sense of patriotism.
- My identity does not come from my job anymore.
- I don't really even have a sense of commitment to family as part of my essential identity. My family birthed and raised me, and I go into therapy and talk about how they traumatized me. Many people don't have a sense of identity, even with their family.

So, what's my identity? I'm looking for my deeper identity—so what's left? Well, after we've deconstructed all the identities in postmodernity, what's the one thing left? Boy/girl. Then postmodernity comes and says, *let's deconstruct that because that identity is not true either.*

So now when a boy or a girl is fifteen years old and they want to have an identity rebellion—they want to go through an appropriate adolescent identity crisis—**the only identity left to rebel against is boy/girl.**

There's nothing left except gender. Then what I do is try to deconstruct my boy/girl identity, but not because I should. The Universe did not make a mistake with most people. There are some people who legitimately should change genders, and we honor and bless that impulse. But for ninety-nine percent of the world, *you were born in the right gender. It wasn't a mistake or a cosmic accident.*

If I want to rebel against my identity, and the only identity left is gender, then I attempt to deconstruct the physicalness of my boy/girl identity. It's happening all over the country. We are saying that people have a right to do that, and that parents have an obligation to support it when necessary. But so often it's completely confused.

The transgender movement is asking the right question but doesn't have a response.

HOMO AMOR: UNIQUE GENDER, MY UNIQUE COMBINATION OF LINE AND CIRCLE QUALITIES

Let's go back to the fundamental question: *what's underneath my boy/girl*?

- Underneath my boy/girl is *Homo amor.*
- Underneath my boy/girl, I'm a Unique Self.

Who am I? I am an irreducibly unique expression of the LoveIntelligence and LoveBeauty, that's the initiating and animating energy of All-That-Is, that lives in me, as me, and through me. That's who I am. As a Unique Self, I'm playing my instrument and participating in the Unique Self Symphony.

- *It's beyond he or she*, as the Gospel of Thomas writes.
- It's beyond man or woman.
- It's my unique combination of line and circle qualities as a unique emergent.

The transgender movement is articulating a holy and sacred impulse. For some people—and I want to honor them so deeply—that impulse might mean changing genders. But for ninety-nine percent of people, it doesn't. It means to realize your deeper identity underneath gender:

I am Reality having a me experience, which is a combination and integration of my line and circle qualities. That's shocking.

There's a deeper identity beneath it all. Who am I?

I'm *Homo amor.* I'm Unique Gender. **Our intention is to be *Homo amor*, to integrate my powerful line and circle as a woman and my powerful line and circle as a man, and to stand with each other as Unique Selves.** That's gorgeous! That's *Homo amor.*

UNIQUE GENDER OF HOMO AMOR

Our intention in reclaiming love as religion, and in moving towards a pragmatic politics of Love, is to embrace the sacred impulse in every movement—to embrace the sacred knowing that the transgender movement is teaching us. And then we go deeper to Unique Gender.

You cannot be *Homo amor* without being Unique Gender. If you're stuck as a woman only in your woman-ness, but you can't access your line (masculine) qualities, or you're stuck as a man, but you can't access your circle (feminine) qualities, then you can't be *Homo amor.* **Homo amor is Unique Gender.** It's so beautiful.

The Unique Gender issue is so important because there's attraction—not just between man and woman, man and man, or woman and woman. That's the old world of polarity. There's also attraction and allurement as we join genius with each other, as we create intimate communion with each other as Unique Genders. Each of us is a Unique Self, and Unique Selves have their own polarity and attraction to each other. We've got to learn new ways of intimate communion, because intimate communion is the royal road to political revolution and world transformation.

EVOLUTIONARY LOVE CODE: THE ROYAL ROAD TO WORLD TRANSFORMATION

Intimate communion is the royal road to political revolution and world transformation.

What does that mean? What does intimate communion have to do with world transformation? Does it even have anything to do with it at all?

We often think intimate communion is *between you and me*, and political revolution is only *in the public sector*. So what does intimate communion have to do with world transformation?

> *There is no world transformation at this moment in time without intimate communion.*

Intimate communion means:

- *Reality seeks intimacy.* This is literally the new *dharma*. This is the new source code. These are the Evolutionary Love codes.
- Reality is the progressive *deepening* of intimacy.
- Reality is evolution, and evolution is the evolution of intimacy. Intimacy means *when parts come together to create a new whole that's more alive, a new whole that's more Good, more True, and more Beautiful.*

We start with quarks that seek and are allured to intimacy with each other, which results in the creation of subatomic particles; these protons, electrons, and neutrons are allured in intimacy with each other to create atoms, which are allured in intimacy to create molecules—all the way up the evolutionary chain.

Here's the big sentence:

Reality is evolution, and evolution is the yearning for more intimacy, a yearning for a new politics of Love, which means that more and more people are connected, and more and more parts are coming together and creating new wholes.

WHENEVER THERE'S A CRISIS IN EVOLUTION, IT'S A CRISIS OF INTIMACY

Whenever there's a crisis in evolution, it's a crisis of intimacy. What was the major political revolution of modernity? The abolishment of slavery. Slavery, which none of the great religions were successful in eradicating, was a failure of intimacy.

In other words, *say I'm a slave trader. I'm at home with my children whom I love, my daughter and my son, and my wife and my brother, my uncle, a happy family—and yet I'm transporting and selling slaves from Africa or Asia. It's unbelievable! I'm loving my family, and yet I'm not intimate with the slaves who are dying at the bottom of my ship and whom I'm selling like commodities if they survive.*

So in effect, prior to abolition, *grace was only "amazing" when it applied to me and my family.* Just hold this, friends. Every major wisdom tradition, none of the great premodern traditions were able to succeed in legally abolishing slavery in the world and standing against slavery the way we needed to. So we needed "Amazing Grace."

What was "Amazing Grace"? It was a political revolution. This song is about the revolution of intimate communion, where we said, *No one's outside the circle.* Now, just think about this for a second. We're about to play the song "Amazing Grace." But we do not only need "Amazing Grace"

7

because there shouldn't be slaves in the world; we abolished slavery. Yet, there are still thirty-five million sexual and labor slaves in the world today. In the Portland and Seattle area, the nexus where I live, there's more sex trafficking than in any other part of the country.

But it's not just that. There are also 12,000 children who die a day of hunger or hunger-related diseases, while restaurants all over the United States are just throwing out food. That's a total failure of intimacy.

Suffering is always a failure of intimacy. Evil is always a failure of intimacy, when somebody is outside the circle.

We are revolutionaries, and to be a revolutionary means your moral community is the world. That's what it means to be *Homo amor*. That's what "Amazing Grace" means. That's intimate communion that brings political revolution. So let's feel into the words of "Amazing Grace," sung here by Judy Collins.

Let's feel the *Amazing Grace* of intimate communion that brings political revolution.

INTIMATE COMMUNION ACTIVATES UNIQUE GENIUS

I [*Barbara*] had a revelation this morning about how you actually bring intimate communion into political revolution and world transformation. Here is how: I've been talking with a new political party, and they want to feature synergistic democracy as a political party that eventually should rise up to be powerful in the United States. They're going the political route. They're going to have a meeting of 125 supporters, who then will be introduced to synergistic democracy, which they have no idea about. And then what will they want to do on behalf of politics?

But I was thinking of the Church in relation to this—because every single person who wants political transformation has something about that transformation that they're most interested in. There's political transformation in general, but more specifically, it could be: *I care about the environment,* or *I'm really concerned about the education of kids,* or *I think we have to improve our justice system,* or *we need a better media ecosystem,* and so on. So they all go into the various sectors of the Wheel of Co-Creation based on their concern for the new politics—and then what they have to do is communion. We're going to need facilitators who are able to bring them into a state of union.

If you're really interested in world transformation, then you have to get to what I call your "deepest heart's desire." The political impulse is not just a superficial "fixing things up" at this time of radical planetary evolution. Political initiative at a time of world transformation is quite profound because we are not just improving something that doesn't work— we're evolving toward something that has perhaps never been seen before.

How would you fully do that? By tapping into your deepest heart's desire, in communion, into a political environment where it's possible to do "vocational arousal" and find each other; then the members of this new party get to be in a love affair. In other words, they get to love each other, and they get to express what they love most. **Love is attractive. They're attracted, so they *become* attractive.**

Intimate communion means you have to be really deep in sharing with each other, as in the Holy of Holies, where we can say anything. We can also say what we care about, if our feelings are hurt, or if we want to try something new, whatever it is. Intimate communion is the royal road.

So you have to be a king or queen, in the best sense of the word, and have a sense of dignity, a sense of your own authority to dare to do it. It's not about trying to get along with others but about being a co-author of your own creation. So there's a lot in that code: Intimate communion is the royal road to political revolution and world transformation.

Just imagine that this group I was talking to yesterday takes the royal road to transformation by identifying its own passion to create among its members, who are doing not just voting based on win/lose metrics but actually creating something new. **We are here for a political revolution and a world transformation. The expression and fulfillment of that intimacy and love is extremely contagious.** You become so attractive when you can do that…

We're always speaking about the intelligence of nature. I believe the intelligence of nature comes through more clearly through us when we're joining genius and moving towards something that we truly care about, more than anything else that there could be. It's obvious that your deepest heart's desire and your unique genius are where the hidden code of intelligence exists in you. Most of the time, it doesn't fully come out.

I would like to review this communion from the point of view of actual, transformative social and political action. **Intimate communion— meaning that it's absolutely essential you know the inner impulse of the other to express and be who you are—is the royal road.** That means everyone is a Unique Self, and nobody is subservient in this mode. That's the nature of evolutionary uniqueness.

I'll just conclude by saying that political revolution and world transformation come through the process of intimate communion, in which we then choose to act together in a way that activates our unique genius. By joining genius, you love each other—and as you love each other, more of your intelligence comes out and you become a better *evolutionary*, a deeper Unique Self, and an Outrageous Lover.

SYNERGISTIC DEMOCRACY AS A UNIQUE SELF SYMPHONY

Oh, my God! Barbara, that was beautiful. Intimate communion creates political revolution, and when we love each other, we see each other. To love is to see; love is a perception. What do I see?

I see your unique gorgeousness, and I see your unique gift

I know that my unique gift needs your unique gift. **I know that together we can synergize the new intimacy of Cosmos.**

But here's the pragmatic politics of Love. We come together not just with top-down corporations and governments, which are important, where: *I join a board, but I'm not thinking about the whole thing; I'm thinking about the board or the company and how it's going.*

No, I actually begin to become *Homo amor*, where my moral community is the world.

All of us, we join our boards, and we're in the boards of our lives; we're the chairman of the boards of our own lives, and we're giving our unique gifts. Then we say: **I'm part of a Unique Self Symphony. I'm going to find the people near me and we're going to create synergistic democracy. What does that mean? It means we're going to synergize, bring together our gifts, and address the unique needs in our unique circle of intimacy and influence—and we're going to do that all over the world.**

That's Unique Self Symphony.

CHAPTER TWO

EVOLUTIONARY CHURCH AS A MICROCOSM OF SYNERGISTIC DEMOCRACY: THE EVOLUTIONARY IMPULSE & I ARE ONE

Episode 152 — September 7, 2019

HOMO AMOR LIVES AS IF THIS WERE THE LAST DAY OF OUR LIVES

We think we live forever. We think we're just going to go on and on. But we remove from our consciousness the realization that **this world is finite, and there's a day that every one of us will face**—some of us in the distant future, some of us in the not-too-distant future, because we actually don't know when that will be—**the last day of our life**.

The way I want to live my life is the way *Homo amor* lives his/her life. *Homo amor* lives as if today were the last day of our lives. I want to invite you to this intention: not that today should literally be the last day of our lives, but could we all live today *as if* this was the last day of our lives. Could we actually be who we would want to be on that last day?

Now, I want to share with you something that is just stunning, as we set our intention. One of the things that the evolutionary mystics understood is that *in one second, you can change everything*.

When you shift your intention and your interior sense of identity, and you become someone that's wider, deeper,

kinder, and in some sense, larger than you ever were, if you can do that, then *that's who you actually are.* You do it just by stepping into that new being.

When I step into a new beingness, I then literally lift up my entire life.

I want to invite everyone into the beingness that evolution is inviting us into at this jump point in human history.

- We are privileged to live at this moment, which is both terrifying and exhilarating beyond measure.
- We are literally at the jump point.
- We are at a phase shift.
- We are at a place that is like the move from single-celled to multi-celled organisms, in which exponential change is creating a world which we're not going to even recognize.

About forty years ago, you had to rent computing power, and it took six weeks in advance to get fifteen minutes on a huge mainframe computer. Now you have an iPhone in your pocket, and it's a thousand times stronger than that mainframe computer, much smaller, and much less expensive.

It doesn't take a city block; it's in your pocket and you have access to it. That iPhone itself is soon going to be the size of a blood cell that will actually be part of your system.

Our entire sense of identity—what it means to be a human being, what it means to have a job, and our location in the Cosmos—is changing.

We're awakening at a moment where we can become truly *Homo amor.* We can become truly a universal species, where we're aware that life is undoubtedly existent in the larger galaxy, and we can begin to re-understand ourselves.

Let me say it differently. It's not just that we begin to re-understand ourselves. It's only *if* we re-understand ourselves; it's only *if* we step into that wider identity that we're actually going to have a tomorrow.

Evolution is elegant. Evolution says, *I'm going to demand for your survival the exact evolution of consciousness that you need*. But it's not an option.

THE ONLY WAY TO CREATE A TOMORROW IS TO TRANSFORM THE ESSENTIAL SENSE OF WHO WE ARE AS HUMAN BEINGS

In order for us to survive as a species, we have to transcend the win/lose metrics. We have to transcend the success story that's creating an exponential growth curve, which is going to eventually drop off; the success story that's expanding the gap between haves and have-nots, that's proliferating rogue technologies run by non-state actors, and that can actually take us down in a fundamental way.

Because of this gap between haves and have-nots, we live in a world filled with increasing discontent:

- Without any shared narrative
- Without any shared Story
- Without any shared sense of identity
- Without any shared sense of Value
- Without any shared sense of meaning that would prevent the wrong use of those technologies

We live without a shared Story that would prevent the explosions, a shared Story that would bind us to a higher code of duty, honor, and love.

We're at this moment where the only way to create a tomorrow is to literally transform the essential sense of who we are as human beings. **The future is now, and in this very second, the memory of the future is *Homo amor.***

We are enacting, we are being, and we are becoming the new species. **We understand**—from the perspective of evolutionary mysticism—**that if we can become it, then it becomes true.**

- We have to bring it down.
- We have to embody it.
- We have to live it.
- We have to create a new world framework in which a thousand flowers can bloom.

But that framework has to be a shared framework of identity, of Evolutionary Love, a shared framework where I actually understand:

Who am I?

- I am a unique expression of Evolutionary Love.
- I am a unique expression of the evolutionary impulse that is needed by All-That-Is.
- Amor, Love itself—not ordinary love, but actually the Love that's the heart of existence itself—lives and configures in me uniquely.
- I have gifts to give that no one else who ever was, is, or will be can give.
- Evolution is dying, breathless, to receive my gifts.

That's what it means to be *Homo amor*. That's what it means to understand and experience Amor. As Solomon wrote, *its insides are lined with love.*

PRAYER: TURNING TO THE INFINITY OF INTIMACY THAT KNOWS MY NAME

We're about to go into prayer. What do we do in prayer? What does prayer mean? As Immanuel Kant, the great philosopher, said, *a modern person never wants to be caught praying.* But he was thinking about the old notion of prayer, where you turn to a Santa Claus-type figure—and no disrespect to Santa Claus—but you turn to a Santa Claus God in the sky and you say, *I'm going to put in a quarter, or some text, or some prayer, and then you'll give me everything I want.* That's not exactly what prayer is.

You do turn to the Divine and ask for things, but you don't turn to Santa Claus.

You turn to the quality of Cosmos, which:

- Is infinitely personal
- Is ultimately intimate
- Knows your name
- Knows everything about you
- Is the force of physics, chemistry, and all of the quantified and qualified structures of mathematics

You turn to the God whom we call "God in the third person": the exponential hundreds of billions and trillions of complex structures of matter: elegant molecules, complex molecules, cellular structures, and organisms; the entire structure of all the mathematics that imbues and organizes; all of the laws of physics that were all in existence at the moment of the Big Bang, which have since evolved to forms that are beyond imagination, which every supercomputer in the world exponentialized couldn't even *begin* to manifest.

All of that, which we call God in the third person, is sitting in a chair beside you, looking at you: we call that God in the second person, the Infinity of Personhood, the Infinity of Intimacy that knows your name.

The Infinity of Intimacy knows my name and needs my service.

The Infinity of Intimacy knows your name, needs your service, invites your partnership, and says to you: *I love you; I need you.*

God in the second person—the Infinity of Intimacy—turns to me and says, *I love you madly*.

Well, you might say: how do you *know* God loves us madly? How do you know Infinity even cares about us?

Because: what are we doing here? **We're here because Infinity chose to manifest finitude**. And finitude? That's us. We know that the Infinite is intimate and that the Infinite desires intimacy—not because of some complex formula, but because we're here right now.

Infinity turned to us, to finitude, and said:

- I celebrate you, and I love you.
- I love you so much that I'm going to step back and hide some of Myself to allow room for you to be.
- Then I'm going to invite you into partnership with Me, for you to realize that you're actually part of Me and not separate from Me; you're unique expressions of Me.
- Then together I'll let you manifest a world in which every human being is a uniquely gorgeous, uniquely beautiful expression of Eros, a unique configuration of Evolutionary Love.
- Let's build this world together.

So the Infinity of Intimacy turns to every one of us and says, *I love you; I need you*.

First, *I love you*, and *to say I love you is to say I need you*.

Now, in prayer, we turn back to the Infinity of Intimacy, God, Ma'at, Christ, *Adonai Elohim*, Buddhahood, Allah, the Implicate Order (of David Bohm), the Evolutionary Love that animates all Reality that knows your name, etc…

We turn, and we say,

Infinity of Intimacy, wow!

- You're holding me in every second; waves are coming into my body.
- I'm being breathed in every moment.
- Thirty-seven trillion cells are alive and being animated by your love, every single second.

But it's not just *I love you, Infinity of Intimacy*. It's: *I need you.*

- I need you to help me.
- I need you because my aunt is having surgery and I need your help.
- I need you because I want to open my heart and I don't quite know how to do it.
- I need you to help me give my gift to the world.

Prayer is when we turn to the Infinity of Intimacy and we say, *I love you, I need you, help me.* We bring our holy and our broken *Hallelujah* before the altar of the Infinity of Intimacy, and we ask for everything—because prayer affirms the dignity of personal need.

We're now going to Leonard Cohen, and we're going to offer up our holy and broken *Hallelujahs*, and we're going to ask for everything. Let's offer every prayer; no one's on the side, no one's sitting out, no one's waiting for someone else. Let's be in prayer as we listen to "Hallelujah" by Leonard Cohen.

I want to invite everyone to really be with us together—let's hold this and lift this. Let's lift this vehicle, this vessel for the light.

Let's pay attention.

Let's give it so much care and so much love.

EVOLUTIONARY LOVE CODE: EVOLUTION IS INTIMACY IN ACTION

Evolution is intimacy in action.

Homo amor makes a contribution, and *Homo amor* is love in action. *Homo amor*—what Barbara and I also called at one stage, *Homo Amore Universalis*. This is the CosmoErotic Universe in person.

What is the CosmoErotic Universe? It's a word that I use in the *dharma* to say that Reality is actually love, or Evolutionary Love, or allurement— expressed as gravity, expressed as electromagnetic attraction, expressed as the self-actualizing Cosmos that moves from bacteria to Bach, from mud to Mozart, from slime to Shakespeare. **It's a way to say that Reality is** *the* *self-actualizing Cosmos moving to higher and higher levels of freedom, elegant* *order, love, and care.*

We're moving from egocentric care "for just me and my peeps" to ethnocentric care where "I'm loving my larger group" to worldcentric care, as expressed in the song "We Are the World" and events like 1985's Live Aid concert. *We literally are the whole world; we are standing for every human being.*

Ultimately, we move to cosmocentric intimacy and cosmocentric love, where we stand for not just humans but all beings on the planet and for the planet awakening as a beacon for all life, even beyond the galaxy.

When we begin to move to cosmocentric consciousness, we're participating in the trajectory of the evolution of Love and Eros that drives all Cosmos.

Eros at its very core is quarks wanting to come together, and hadrons, leptons, and muons forming a proton, a subatomic particle, and then subatomic particles coming together to form an atom, and then atoms coming together to form a molecule. It's CosmoErotic all the way down and up; we live in a CosmoErotic Universe.

Homo amor is not some weird aberration. It's not some saccharine idea of let me be a sweet and loving person in this dog-eat-dog world because that's really nice. No!

- *Homo amor universalis* is my real, true identity. It's actually what evolution demands at this moment.
- As *Homo amor universalis*, I realize that I am evolution; the impulse and I are one. I am the CosmoErotic Universe in person.
- The universe moves towards intimacy. Evolution is the evolution of intimacy. So I put my *love in action*: **when I do something**—when I call someone, when I open my heart in a way that I couldn't have before, when I reach out and I give my unique gift in my unique circle of intimacy and influence—**then I become evolution; evolution awakens in me.**

Evolution moves from unconscious to conscious evolution, and we begin to synergize as Unique Self Symphonies, and we move towards the goal—the *telos*—of all of Reality: ever-deepening intimacy.

It's the mission of this One World Church, which is a Planetary Awakening in Love through Unique Self Synergies, in which all of us are *Homo amor universalis*, playing our instruments in Unique Self Symphony. We come together, address every need, match needs and resources, and generate a synergistic world of Evolutionary Love.

That's what da Vinci did. Every week, I mention him because he's "soul root" connected to us. He's at the beginning of modernity, and the Black Death had swept through Europe. Da Vinci stepped in with a gang of a thousand people, not more, and they told a new story of human identity. They told a new Universe Story in the Renaissance.

And that's what we're doing now.

HOMO AMOR UNIVERSALIS AS A SPECIES

This Church, by the grace of God, is truly inspired by the evolutionary impulse. The evolutionary impulse is taking a jump—not because we're so great, but because that's what evolution does. It jumps from single-celled to multi-celled to animal to human, and we happen to be living in the jump. But what I think is so awesome for this Church is, rather than being the Church of the Resurrection of the Christ, we're really the Church of the evolution of humanity—with the love of Christ and the Buddha and all the great sages and avatars of the past.

Here's the simple sentence: *I am Homo amor universalis in a CosmoErotic Universe.*

When I say I am Homo amor universalis in a CosmoErotic Universe, then I hold that and deepen into the qualities of being of a person who is that.

It lifts up absolutely every part of my being, and our being, and our Church's being. If I am the CosmoErotic Universe as an expression of the impulse of evolution taking a jump in my generation to a universal species, in a universe probably filled with other life, my own inner impulse will turn on.

The impulse and I are one.

That impulse—for being able to go from nothing at all to everything that is, or from the Big Bang to this big bang in each of us as human individuals—is an awesome spirituality. So we each say that to each other and to

21

ourselves: **I am *Homo amor universalis* in a CosmoErotic Universe, with my vocation turned on at the exact jump point of human history.**

We ask: What is my vocation? Do I dare go the whole way with my vocation and my calling?

After you've explored the vocational, you have to think of it socially. Here we are in the breakdown of democracy as it is currently being practiced almost everywhere. The win/lose form of democracy certainly isn't working. It's done its job.

What's its new form? It is synergistic democracy: a democracy that connects co-creators—individually, nationally, and globally. We know that synergy is much greater than the sum of the parts. If we say that this is a synergistic democracy in this Church, our goal would be that everybody's uniqueness joins with each other's uniqueness in such a way that we're much greater than the sum of our parts.

I see the Evolutionary Church as a microcosm of synergistic democracy. So we're going both individually and personally; we're going vocationally to whatever we feel our calling is, but we're also going deep into social synergy. I don't believe the church has been able to do that very well, at least recently. Maybe the early church did.

So what happens to us interpersonally (not just spiritually or internally) as *Homo amor universalis* if we love each other? Marc and I have come up with the idea of role mates to soul mates to whole mates.

In whole-mate relationships, shared love leads to the blending of sexuality and supra-sexuality, intimacy and supra-intimacy—for the purpose of shared attention directed to a goal that benefits all of humanity. Our personal love affairs as members of *Homo amor universalis* are awesome. I am *Homo amor universalis* with each one of you, as we lift our species to the next stage of evolution.

INTIMACY MEANS: MY MORAL COMMUNITY IS THE PLANET

Who are we? *We are Homo amor.*

We can all say: *I am Homo amor, and I am vocationally aroused to give my unique gift to my unique circle of intimacy and influence, which is Reality itself.*

Because I am the evolution of intimacy, to me, intimacy means: *my moral community is the planet.*

Friends, to do this we all have to play an instrument, and we're all invited. There's no joy, there's no grace, there's no delight, there's no Eros greater than the vibrational arousal and the vocational arousal of being your Unique Self.

- We need new music; we need to write new songs.
- We need new technology.
- We need a new level of care, and love, and ecstasy.
- We need new *dharma.*

I'm going to work on the *dharma* day and night—that's all I do. I'm trying to write, and think, and breathe, and feel these distinctions, and share them all the time.

- Let's work on the technology.
- Let's work on the music.
- Let's work on governance.
- Let's work on the infrastructure.
- Let's work on the medical system.
- Let's work on education.
- Let's do this together.
- We are a synergistic democracy in its microcosmic form, here in the Evolutionary Church. We are a Planetary Awakening in Love through a Unique Self Symphony.

Think Gospel Church in the South, think Martin Luther King—let's all be Martin Luther King together. It was the Gospel Church that linked everyone. Think Evolutionary Churches and One World Churches all over the world, with a million ministers: men, women, transgender, some Martians, beings from different galaxies. But this is this network that links us in a shared *dharma*.

We have a shared Story.

We are each Unique Selves; we are Evolutionary Unique Selves.

We're whole mates joining genius in love to co-create.

CHAPTER THREE

THE DIVINE YES OF INFINITE POSSIBILITY LIVES AND BREATHES IN US: WE ARE EVOLUTION AWAKENING TO ITSELF

Episode 153 — September 14, 2019

RECLAIMING EVOLUTIONARY OUTRAGEOUS LOVE AS RELIGION

We are revolutionaries. This is about an Outrageous Love revolution. But it's not just a slogan or an aphorism. It's a reality.

We're at a moment between utopia and dystopia, a moment between evolution and devolution. We're at a moment which is a literal phase shift in human culture, unlike that which we've ever seen before, where we can either devolve, or we can claim the true nature of Reality as the Universe: A Love Story.

We can recognize that we live in a CosmoErotic Universe. We can know that we are not just *Homo sapiens sapiens*; we are *Homo amor*.

This requires the emergence of a new identity, an actual transformation of identity.

The transformation of identity is the creation of a new configuration of intimacy, meaning we become intimate with parts of us that have been split off.

We want to engage and reclaim the parts of us that have been split off from our identity. But what's been split off is not just—as they teach in shadow integration seminars—your jealousy, or your rage, or your anger. No, those are shadow qualities. **What's really in shadow is our greatness.**

So we have to confess our greatness. We have to confess that actually, we don't yearn for ordinary love—which is a strategy of the ego and seeks to give us some status in a world filled with unrest—as beautiful as ordinary love is. **Rather, we yearn for Outrageous Love; we are incarnations of Outrageous Love.**

Outrageous Love is not mere human sentiment, Outrageous Love is the heart of existence itself. We are reclaiming love as religion, as we move towards a pragmatic politics of Evolutionary Love and Outrageous Love.

We need to reclaim—at the center of change—the impulse of religion, which is knowing that the world is meaningful, that the world matters, and that we're personally implicated in the story.

Sometimes we get lost in the ideas of the Human Potential Movement and forget that seventy percent of the world lives in an organized religion and that we live in a global world. So if we can't feel the pulse of religion, if we can't speak to that, then we can't transform the world. We get lost in our own very narrow silos of human development talking to each other, and we can't create the movement that we want to create.

We are here to make a revolution! That is our intention. We are articulating Evolutionary Love codes that are structural to the very structure and nature of Reality itself. This is the new *dharma*. We're writing together, if you will, a new scripture. We are da Vinci. We are Muhammad. We are Moses. We are the people. We are simple laborers working in our fields in this vineyard. We are Reich, and we are Jung on his best day.

We are coming together to tell a new story. Because it's only telling that new story—with passionate, ecstatic urgency, with deep spaciousness, with radical integrity—**that can move us into creating heaven on earth and liberate us from the imminent suffering experienced by billions of people**—particularly the most vulnerable—**that is rapidly intensifying as the various dimensions of existential risk play themselves out.**

Oh my God, what a delight to be here!

LOVING YOUR WAY TO ENLIGHTENMENT: PRAYER AS EXPONENTIALIZED INTIMACY

We are setting our intention for prayer, and we are participating in the evolution of prayer. Every week we come together to pray and we say three things. **Prayer affirms the dignity of personal need because the Infinity of Intimacy knows my name.** *I'm not invisible.* **So when you pray, you ask for everything.**

God is not only the Infinity of Power, the third-person Divine, if you will. God is not only the pulsing course of physics moving through Cosmos.

And God not only wildly and ecstatically and stunningly lives in me, which is God in first person. *Tat tvam Asi: Thou art that.* Divinity lives and courses through me. Those are two critical faces of the Divine talked about in the *Zohar*, the great thirteenth-century mystical text, and by Kashmir Shaivism.

But there's another dimension of God, what we call God in the second person, which is *the Infinity of Intimacy that knows my name.*

In meditation, if you can, find your most ecstatic, intimate moment. It might be a moment of quivering tenderness beyond imagination; it might be with a lover or a beloved, a friend, a son or a daughter, or a brother or a sister. It doesn't matter who it's with. It's this moment of true intimacy where there's no distance, and when you feel the Beloved yearning to hold you, yearning to nourish you, yearning to ravish you.

In intimacy, there's this desire.

- It can be a desire that is classically erotic.
- It can be a desire that is classically tender in Eros.
- It can be sexual.
- It can be non-sexual.
- It can be purely, stunningly, sweetly, gorgeously nurturing and nourishing.

But all of those are faces of Eros. When Rumi talks about the Beloved, that Beloved is all of those dimensions.

RECLAIMING PRAYER: THE SECOND-PERSON FACE OF THE INFINITY OF INTIMACY

Right now, find your most tender moment, your most sensually erotic moment, where you felt the full force of the Beloved's desire focused on you, and you knew that life was self-evidently good. Now, magnify that, amplify that, exponentialize that.

Feel that second face of God, that Infinity of Power who is the Infinity of Intimacy that pulses for you, that yearns for you, that knows your name, desperately wanting to hold you so tenderly and ravish you so fully, when you know that life is self-evidently good and all the questions melt away.

That is what we call "loving your way to enlightenment." That is the interior face of Cosmos. That's not dogma—that's the *dharma*. That's the best understanding we currently have based on the realizations of the interior and exterior sciences.

So when we pray, we turn to that Infinity of Intimacy and we say:

Oh my God, can I bring everything before you? I want to ask for everything, and I want to share all of me with you. Can you imagine a place I can share all of me? *I'm going to bring my holy and my broken Hallelujah.*

Our friends in Judaism, Christianity, Islam, and certain forms of Shintoism, and certain forms of Confucianism, all talk about this. Let's take the Christian example: *I can rest in Christ; Christ holds me.* See, they're not wrong. The fundamentalists didn't get it entirely wrong. And the sophisticated New Age version—*God is the power of the universe, neutral forces of physics*—is also a dimension of the Divine.

We need to reclaim God in the second person and free the beauty of that truth from a fundamentalist, ethnocentric, homophobic reading of it. God in the second person has been hijacked by a fundamentalist church. But we need to honor that intuition—that realization—and reclaim prayer.

Because we're not alone.

We sometimes live lives of quiet desperation, but you can never genuinely live a life of lonely desperation—because you're never alone. She's always waiting. She's always waiting to receive the holy and broken Hallelujah and to look at us and scream YES.

God/Goddess is screaming YES to the goodness of our existence.

So let's pray as we listen to "Hallelujah" by Leonard Cohen.

Hallelujah, which in Hebrew means both broken intoxication and pristine praise. Brothers and sisters around the world, fellow revolutionaries, fellow Outrageous Lovers reclaiming Love as religion—not ordinary love, but Outrageous Love—it's time to pray.

To pray means I'm vulnerable. To pray means I confess not only my greatness but my vulnerability, and I ask for everything.

- ◆ We're all vulnerable.
- ◆ We're all imperfect vessels for the light.
- ◆ We're all fabulous and gorgeous.
- ◆ We're all fragile.

Let's pray. And when we pray, we ask for everything. We offer tears of joy, tears of ecstasy, tears of relief. This is the true nature of Reality, and we can find this true nature. Like da Vinci did, we're going to tell this new story. Let's lift these prayers to the sky. Let's wrap them together and impress them on the lips of God. We can't be afraid to talk of God—the God that lives in us and breathes in us. We pray to the God who is the Infinity of Intimacy.

EVOLUTIONARY LOVE CODE: INFINITY SCREAMS AN ECSTATIC "YES!"

Infinity desires finitude.

The desire for intimacy screams YES. Infinity cries out YES to finitude.

The Big Bang, the great Flaring Forth, is the erotic and ecstatic YES of the Infinity of Intimacy, the radical goodness, truth, and beauty of existence itself.

Our code this week is YES. The Infinite is intimate. Infinity desires finitude. These are the new codes of the new world; these are the new codes of the New human and the new humanity. The desire for intimacy that drives Cosmos screams YES. **Infinity cries out YES to finitude; the unmanifest cries out YES to the manifest.** The Big Bang, the great Flaring Forth, is the erotic, ecstatic, evolutionary YES of the Infinity of Intimacy, affirming the radical goodness, truth, and beauty of existence itself and of each one of us. So our word is YES.

Let's go back to the Bible for a second—and we're also going to go back to Confucius and Buddhism, and going to go forward to evolutionary science and complexity theory, chaos theory—to reclaim the best of the Biblical tradition.

The Bible has a word, kein, which means "integrity." But kein also means YES.

MY YES IS AN INCARNATION OF THE HOLY YES OF THE BIG BANG

There's a movie called *The Garden of the Finzi-Continis* about this Italian aristocratic family and about what happens in the Holocaust when they're in a concentration camp, stripped of clothes, and there's no networking to do. That's when it becomes clear who has a real YES. We sometimes disguise our NO in all sorts of marketing language, all sorts of New Age language, all sorts of Human Potential language, and all sorts of religious language. We've got to strip that away. **We have to get to the deepest heart of who we are, which is a YES.**

My YES is an incarnation of the holy YES of the Big Bang. Just like at the moment of the Big Bang, Divinity, the Infinity of Intimacy, manifested and unfolded the Possibility of Possibility. The Divine YES has infinite possibility, and that Divine YES literally breathes me and lives me.

31

- I am evolution awakening to itself.
- I am a unique configuration of intimacy and desire.
- I am moving beyond *Homo sapiens*—I am *Homo amor universalis.*
- I am the leading edge of evolution's desire.
- My desire and my unrest are divine unrest, and my YES is God's YES.

Let's look at each other and say to each other: *Oh my God, YES! I feel your joy, and I feel your pain, and I feel your pathos.*

INTIMACY: SHARED IDENTITY AND MUTUALITY

Intimacy means we move beyond exclusive identification with the skin-encapsulated ego. Intimacy means shared identity in the context of otherness, plus mutuality of recognition, mutuality of feeling, mutuality of value, mutuality of purpose, mutuality of pathos.

- *I feel you…*
- *And you feel me…*
- *And I feel you feeling me…*
- *And you feel me feeling you feeling me…*
- *And together, we cry out, YES!*

And sometimes I say NO in order to say a bigger YES, so that NO is part of the YES.

- YES to my greatness.
- YES to embracing my vulnerability.
- YES to giving my unique gift.
- YES to taking my place on the stage of history—building together a revolution that will become a force for healing and transformation, unlike that which the world has ever seen, as we reclaim Love as religion.
- YES to my unique gift that no one who ever was, is, or will

be—but me—can give.

- ◆ YES to the dimension of me that can stand at the abyss, at the edge of darkness, and say, *Let there be light*—a unique configuration and pulsing of light unlike that which can be shone by any other being who ever was, is, or will be.
- ◆ YES to the goodness.
- ◆ YES to the realization that *I'm intended by Cosmos, I'm needed by Cosmos, I'm chosen by Cosmos, I'm recognized by Cosmos, I'm adored by Cosmos.*

My growth and transformation is the growth and transformation of All-That-Is. That's the YES, my friends.

It's the YES that initiates Reality.

It's the YES that emerges from us.

AFFIRMING THE BIG YES AS THE IMPULSE OF EVOLUTION

I want to affirm in every one of us the big YES. What is it that we most deeply want to say YES to, within ourselves? That if we say YES to it the whole way, we go the whole way in this lifetime. **The desire to say the big YES takes courage.**

What I've been discovering in working with people around the theme of the big YES is that people often have a hidden YES deep inside them, but they don't want to say it. The reason they don't want to is that they might then be committed to it. What if they say the big YES and they fail? It might not work. It might defeat their sense of well-being.

When we say the big YES to the Infinite Intimacy of our yearning to create, we're saying YES to God, YES to Source, YES to the Christ energy within all of us. When we say YES to that, with no conflict in our YES, daring to give the big YES, then something completely magical begins to happen.

It's as though the process of creation created us and gave us freedom to say YES or not say YES; everybody has that freedom.

Say YES to the deepest impulse within you: to express, to be, to love, to get into the world.

I want to say the big YES for my love and participation in the Evolutionary Church with all of you. That holy YES in me is the impulse of creation and the impulse of evolution, going through our hearts, in unison with everybody uniquely in this Church, offering to a culture, which is either rapidly approaching devolution or conscious evolution.

Let this Church be a vehicle for the YES of humanity: to love more, create more, and give more together.

Let the Evolutionary Church be the vehicle for the evolution of love in the world. Let's just imagine, for the moment, this Church having that capability of reaching everyone in their YES. Because how would it be that there would be love throughout the world? All the individual humans with this creative impulse who hold it back, or don't quite dare to say it, now say YES together.

Let's imagine the chorus of YES, stimulated by all of us saying YES together right now. Because our YESs are joining, our YESs are synergizing, and our YESs are, therefore, far more empowered than the individual YESs of any of us.

This is the power of being in the Evolutionary Church together. Let's together experience the Infinity of Intimacy in our YES to the impulse of creation in each of us. I believe there are over 10,000 people who have so far, in some way, indicated their desire to say YES.

I was reading from the New Testament when Jesus dared to say: *It's in every one of us.* He dared to say that the resurrection was because of the new human emerging in evolution, and he demonstrated for us what we are becoming. In the Evolutionary Church, we are saying YES to the Christ energy, we're saying YES to Buddha, and YES to all the great saints.

But in this particular instance, let's make the Resurrection the evolution of all of humanity. Let's make the Resurrection the total creation of the Infinity of Intimacy, where the genius of humanity will be given forth into the world. Let's make this Evolutionary Church a statement—perhaps for the first time, from the point of view of evolution—to fulfill the impulse, not only in each one of us, but each one of us synergized to fulfill the impulse of the whole system together.

In the Evolutionary Church, we say YES. **But we don't say YES just as an individual; we say YES as an individuated expression of the impulse itself.** *When you say YES once all the way, then everything changes.* The way to actually transform is to take my seat at the table and say YES all the way.

So here's a question. Are you willing to play a larger game? That's the first question. Are we willing to say YES to that?

- Are we willing to participate in the evolution of love? There's no greater question in the world.
- Are you willing to know that you're personally implicated in the evolution of love?
- Are you willing to go the whole way in this lifetime and to make a contribution?
- Are you willing to make a real contribution of *my heart, my mind, my resources, my very soul*?
- Are we willing to say to each other, *there's nothing for you that I wouldn't do*?
- Are we willing to know that it's One Love and it's One Heart, and it's One Body and it's One Desire—evolutionary desire?

There's only one question: *How deep is your love?* That's the only question. How deep can I go? Can I go from ordinary love to Outrageous Love and Evolutionary Love?

Can I feel the very Love that initiated Reality, alive in me? Because that's the truth.

That's what it means to love our way to enlightenment.

CHAPTER FOUR

EVOLUTIONARY FAMILIA: INTIMACY GENERATES EMERGENCE

Episode 154 — September 21, 2019

WE ARE AT A PIVOTING POINT IN HISTORY

Are you willing to play a larger game? We are reclaiming Love as religion and moving towards a pragmatic politics of Love: in this place of revolution, in this place of evolutionary emergence, in this place at the leading edge of evolution at a critical moment poised between utopia and dystopia.

Let's see if we can, just for a moment, move out of ourselves—out of our privilege, out of all of the social mobility that's defined our lives, out of our socioeconomic classes, whatever they may be—**and actually feel the world.**

Feel the world, and feel the force of what I call the "second shock of existence." The first shock of existence was when the human being realized, *I'm going to die.* But it wasn't just the realization of an animal. It was the first consciousness of death, which likely took place as we moved from a hunter-gathering society and into early horticulture and agriculture.

The first shock of existence: *I'm going to die.* **The only way to respond to that shock was to unleash a depth of Spirit, a depth of goodness, truth, and beauty, which was the beginning of all the world's spiritualities.**

But now, after the journey, and after all of the stages so far, we've come shockingly to this moment between utopia and dystopia, and we're now facing the second shock of existence. **The second shock of existence is the possibility of the death not of the individual human but the death of humanity.** The death of humanity is a genuine possibility if we don't respond to the ten or more interrelated forms of existential risk (risks to our very existence) that confront the planet. That's a big deal.

At the same time, we also have this possibility of utopia—this possibility of creating heaven on earth, this possibility for humanity that's never before existed. We're at this moment of possibility, both for devolution and evolution. We're at what Rilke called a "pivoting point." We're before the second shock of existence, which could either end us or be the beginning of an unimaginably glorious future.

What's going to take us home? What's going to make the difference? What is the pivotal move?

What's the most highly leveraged move that we can make at the pivoting point, that will unleash our potency, power, and poignancy of what it means to be human?

The answer is really simple. The answer is that we step up and we play a larger game. Are you willing to play a larger game? Are you willing to take the lid off? Are you willing to go the whole way in this lifetime? Who's willing to go the whole way in this lifetime? Give me a *YES, I am.* We're willing to go the whole way in this lifetime—all the way, with nothing left out. Are you willing to participate in the evolution of love?

That means to tell a new story.

A NEW UNIVERSE STORY IS A NEW INTIMACY IN WHICH THE WHOLE IS GREATER THAN THE SUM OF THE PARTS

When da Vinci was in Florence and the Black Death ravaged Europe, da Vinci couldn't go to every hamlet in Europe and feed people and bring healing. The medicine wasn't available. The means weren't available. The transportation wasn't available. There were no more than about a thousand people, as Paul Tillich pointed out, who were genuinely involved at the heart of the Renaissance.

What did they do? They told a new story.

They brought together the best of the interior sciences and the best of the exterior sciences—and they wove them together into a new intimacy.

A new intimacy means a new configuration of parts in which the whole that emerges is greater than the sum of its parts. That's a new Universe Story. Out of that emerges a new story of identity, a new sexual narrative, a new narrative of power, a new narrative of community. That new story raised all boats.

THE GAP BETWEEN EXTERIOR AND INTERIOR IMAGINATION

The new story of the Renaissance was incomplete. It developed very intensively in the exterior sciences and it unleashed technology beyond imagination.

But a gap was formed as the interior sciences stopped their evolution.

A gap formed between the ability to literalize exterior imagination—technology in its classical sense—and our ability to literalize interior imagination.

There was a collapse of interior imagination. Interior imagination had taken a leap, and then it stopped. After the Renaissance, that leap was enormous, unbelievable beyond imagination:

- The leap produced democracy.
- The leap produced feminism.
- The leap produced human rights, so there was an assertion of human dignity.

But then it stopped. **The leap of interior imagination stopped articulating and evolving a vision of identity.**

We did not ask ourselves the following questions:

- Once we have rights, what do we do with them?
- What are our responsibilities?
- What are our noble obligations and invitations?
- What is our quest?

So the literalizing of interior imagination stalled. It became about rights, but it lost a vision of rapture. It lost a vision of what it means to be a human being. *I have rights so I can be middle class*—which is fantastic, and the whole world wants to be middle class, because it's one of the greatest innovations of humanity.

But then what do I do? Once I've met Maslow's survival needs, what do I do next?

We need to move beyond Maslow's hierarchy of needs and even beyond self-actualization, which is the actualization of the Separate Self. In other words, we fulfilled our human rights, but we didn't know what to do with them. We got lonely, alienated, and lost our sense of purpose.

The exterior technology ran wild. But what about interior technology?

- What does it mean to be a human being?
- What's the purpose of my life?
- Why am I here?
- What does it mean to love?
- How do I love?
- How do I create intimacy?
- What is a new vision of intimacy?

All of that got lost. Now we're facing, as a direct result, this explosion of exterior imagination, alongside a breakdown of interior imagination.

Precisely in that gap, we face the second shock of existence.

So why are we here?

- We are here as revolutionaries.
- We are here as evolutionaries.
- We are here as Outrageous Lovers.
- We are here as the emergence of *Homo amor* to tell this new story.
- We are urgent, spacious, relaxed, and ecstatic.
- We are filled with charisma, which means that we feel the Spirit moving through us.
- We feel called, and we're here to answer that call together and love each other madly.

WE MUST RECLAIM GOD

We're about to enter into prayer. What are we doing in prayer? It's about understanding that *the god you don't believe in doesn't exist.* But God is more real than anything you can imagine.

God is, God lives, God is alive—and we're not afraid of the word God.
We specifically don't use other words, which is a kind of beautiful and lovely New Age custom, I understand. It came about because we wanted to avoid resistance to the word God, which had so much baggage.

But here at the One World Church, we're reclaiming words like church, synagogue, and mosque, and we're reclaiming words like religion and God. Even though we know—precisely because we know—that they have both glorious and corrupt histories, and many of us spent our lives trying to move beyond them. But if we want to create a One World, we have to talk to the *whole* world. Sixty-five to seventy percent of the world is in direct relationship with God, and they use the word God. So we can't avoid the word. We have to participate together in the evolution of God:

- God is the no-thing, the Source.
- God is the Atman that is Brahman.
- God is the animated, pulsing evolutionary impulse.
- God is Real.

THE THREE FACES OF GOD

1. God lives both in me, as me, and through me. That's God in the first person.
2. God speaks to me directly. God holds me. That's God in the second person.
3. God is the force of Cosmos, Consciousness, and Outrageous Love. God is the pulsing energy of physics and chemistry, all the physical laws, and the four fundamental forces: the strong and weak nuclear, the electromagnetic, and the gravitational. That's God in the third person.

Those forces of the Cosmos, the forces that explode supernovas, are but a fraction of the God force: That's third person. First person: It's moving in me, It's alive in me, It's speaking through me. Second person: God is holding me.

In prayer, we touch all three.

To create a world conversation, we've got to create a shared spiritual language which includes all three faces of God. We must reclaim God.

1. The academy and Western liberals only talk, if at all, about God in third person, the impersonal third-person force that moves through Cosmos. That's as far as we can get.
2. Then the churches say: *It's also God in second person, but it's my God. God is speaking to me, and God is only speaking to me. My religion is the religion; we're the chosen people, and you're on the outside.* As Augustine said, *there's no redemption outside of the church*, and he meant *his* church.
3. Then there's God in first person: spoken about by all sorts of mysticism, both East and West. *God lives in me. God is moving and alive in me.* This has also been adopted by the New Age and Human Potential Movements.

But each group ignores the others. The academy says science is God in the third person, but they ignore the second-person intimate God speaking to me, and the first-person God alive in me. (In fact, the scientist is actually moved by God in the first person: the creative, intuitive impulse that animates us. The scientist says, *I don't know where God is*, when the entire enterprise of science is God in the first person.)

In order to create a new language, reweave the source code, and participate in the evolution of the source code, we need to introduce these three faces of God: first person, second person, and third person.

Particularly in prayer, we can reclaim that which is most missing: the God who loves me madly, who knows my name. As Rumi said, *I want to fall into the arms of the Beloved.* Let's add to Rumi: I want to bring my holy and broken *Hallelujah* before the Divine and offer up all of my brokenness and heartbreak, my contraction, and my crises of intimacy.

EVERY CRISIS AT ITS CORE IS A CRISIS OF INTIMACY

Every crisis, at its core, is a crisis of intimacy. We're living in the middle of a global intimacy disorder, and all crises between us are crises of intimacy. So we've got to start by becoming intimate with the whole thing and intimate with each other.

We do that first by turning to the Divine. We say: *God, Beloved, can I tell you everything? Can I share everything with you?*

Then we hear the divine whisper, God who is the Infinity of Intimacy, who says, *Tell me everything*. That's the holy and the broken *Hallelujah*.

We come to pray, and when we pray—with tears in my eyes, my friends—we ask for everything. Prayer affirms the dignity of personal need.

In prayer, I turn to God who's not only the Infinity of Power, but God who is the Infinity of Intimacy who knows my name.

Can you imagine what that means? Can we step out? Imagine we're doing this. We're participating together in the evolution of love, we're evolving the source code together, and as we can feel it here, all of Reality begins to be able to feel it. Imagine what that means.

God/Goddess, the Infinity of Intimacy, knows my name and says: *Ask for everything.*

So we pray. "Hallelujah, " by Leonard Cohen.

Let's feel this.

Let's intimately weave these prayers together.

Let's lift them to the sky.

WHAT'S GOING TO MAKE THE DIFFERENCE IS INTIMACY

We're at this moment in history. We're the One World Church. What does that mean? Synagogue, church, mosque, secular atheist center, and more. Meaning we're holding the *dharma*, we're holding the codes, we're holding the New Story.

What's going to make this work? What's going to make the difference between succeeding and not succeeding?

We're at this moment in history where we have to come together. What's going to make all the difference is intimacy.

It's all about how we love each other and how we create between us, in this Church, a Field of Intimacy.

EVOLUTIONARY LOVE CODE: GOD IS THE INFINITY OF INTIMACY; INTIMACY GENERATES EMERGENCE

The god you don't believe in doesn't exist.

God is the Infinity of Intimacy equals God is the Possibility of Possibility.

To change the trajectory of your life, you cannot repeat yesterday's intimacy. Idolatry is to worship at the altar of yesterday's intimacy.

Today's intimacy transcends and includes yesterday's intimacy but adds new parts that never were before.

Intimacy generates emergence.

GENERATING A FIELD OF INTIMACY

A Field of Intimacy always means a Field of Forgiveness. A Field of Intimacy means that no matter what, we always stay in, and we never look away. **We can come closer or step back, open or close, go on our autonomous journey, or step towards communion. But we never look away.** There are no words that can't be spoken gently and tenderly.

There are always key nodes in history when we can create heaven on earth—and we've never before seen a node like the one we're in now. We're at this incredible moment, poised between utopia and dystopia. But in every one of these moments—and exponentially, especially in this one—*what's going to make the difference is intimacy:* the intimacy of the field between us, which is always where things break down.

I was speaking at a church of a friend of mine a couple of years ago in LA, one of the most famous churches in the country. He said to me, *Marc, it's a total mess here. When Sunday service is over, what's happening in this place is like a political nightmare.* That happens everywhere. Churches, business-es, NGOs (non-governmental organizations)—the politics between and within them, the anger, the contraction, the people not telling the truth, the people not owning their shadows, and the failure to create an actual fabric of Love. It fails time and again.

One of the things we're committed to here is a Field of Love; it's a Field of Love unlike any other. We've got to love each other and find each other.

- We've got to step in and sometimes step back.
- We must never look away.
- We've got to forgive.
- We've got to always be in exchange, sitting across from each other, looking at each other face to face, listening deeply.
- You always have to be the one to say, *I got that wrong, I apologize. I'm so sorry, let me try that again.*

I've seen it in my life at least five different times, where there was something major that could happen in the world that could change the course of history for the better, *and it broke down because of the inability to create genuine intimacy between human beings.* I've seen three different moments where movements could have erupted and shaken the planet with a glorious *Hallelujah* and changed so many lives—but it broke down because of the contractions of personal ego. **Only personal Outrageous Love heals the contraction of personal ego,** which is so desperate to prove that it exists, and so it plays this comparative game by making somebody else small. That's not the game we need to play.

We're moving towards a Planetary Awakening in Love through Unique Self Symphonies. We're creating an Evolutionary Family but not a dysfunctional family. We evolve the family system, the *familia.* We treat each other with such honor and respect.

We make mistakes sometimes, but we're making mistakes in the right direction. There's nothing that can't be fixed or transformed, and there's no wound that remains untransformed. It's that Field of Intimacy that we generate between us that are the wings.

In mysticism, it's the *Merkabah,* the chariot; that's the only chariot we can ride on. We have to create a model of Evolutionary Family but a family that is next level, a family in which we are all brothers and sisters, and we say to each other: *There's nothing for you that I wouldn't do.*

INTIMACY MEANS IT'S NOT MINE—IT'S OURS

I'm going to tell you just a strange, personal confession. I've given away hundreds of thousands of dollars in my life, and I don't have a lot of money. When I get money, I usually give it away: $30,000 to this person, help that person buy a house, help that person, this person. **Whenever money flows to me, I give it away. Why? Because it's not mine. It was never mine to start with. That's what intimacy means.**

Intimacy means, it's not mine. *It's mine, it's mine, I'm holding on to it.* No, it's not mine. It's ours.

The whole notion that it's "my" life—why would you think that? Why is it *your* life?

- Did you decide where to be born?
- Did you decide what socioeconomic class you'd be born into?
- Did you decide when to be born?
- Did you decide the nature of your interior persona? I'm pretty sure all those decisions were made without you.
- Do you decide when to die? No, you don't. That decision is also made without you.

What have you got? You've got this moment in between. In this moment in between, you can realize:

- I came here not because I made a decision, but *because I was being lived by a greater Life.*
- I'm going to leave here—not because it's my decision, but because I'm being lived by a greater Life in this moment of my death, which is the moment of my transition.

In this lifetime, I wake up and create a Field of Intimacy where I'm giving my unique gifts and my unique love. I am loving Reality open and stepping into the place where I can play my instrument, in what Barbara and I called *a planetary awakening in love through a Unique Self Symphony.*

THE POWER OF INTIMACY IN OUR EMERGENCE

God is the Possibility of Possibility; God in the first person. "In the beginning was the Word, and the Word was made God." First there's consciousness, which then becomes the consciousness-force that creates everything, including us. There are all of those great visions of the almighty Creator.

We, who are created by the almighty Creator, are now aware that that Creator has come in as and through us: to observe us, to be intimate with us, to communicate with us, to live through us, and to be as us. It's not only that God has come in and has been able to activate me and you. First of all, contact that force that turns you on—how do we know what to do? How do we activate our lives when God comes in? We have to listen deeply. I have to pray and listen or write in my journal every day about it, in order to ask, *Tell me what this means, God.* Then I listen, then I get it, and then I do it.

> *When it becomes intimate,*
> *God becomes who we are.*

The thing that's very interesting to imagine is that God is noticing us right now. Do you feel intimate with this force that is God as you, creating greater possibilities in this moment? Now God is doing this, and we're noticing ourselves as communicators of God, doing all of this right now. What does that do personally, if you can experience it?

Just experience this directly, as God being intimate as you in this moment, creating a new trajectory—for your life, my life, and our life—through this intimacy.

God in the second person is directly communicating with me, and I am incarnating that "YES!" I'm changing the trajectory of my life. Let's take a moment to see if, internally, you and I are personally changing the trajectory of our lives because of this divine intimacy that we are now experiencing together, since intimacy generates emergence.

This is the way the Great Church started originally. I'm sure they had collective intimacy, and so they collectively experienced it and made it happen. What we're doing right now in the Church of Evolutionary Love is collectively changing the trajectory of this Church. **We're changing the trajectory of this Church to be a voice of the intimacy of God in**

everyone, changing the trajectory—not only of their personal lives but of lives on the planet.

Our crisis is a birth. We now have the trajectory of that intimacy in each of us, collectively in this Church.

I want to integrate into every one of us the awesome reality that this is true and that we are now affecting the entire system, as all great moments of history have done in the past. Right now, we're at the greatest point of evolution—by choice, not by chance, for the very first time—collectively. This Church, as far as I know, is the first one in the world to bring God intimately as the trajectory of our own personal lives towards a Planetary Awakening in Love in a Unique Self Symphony that turns the entire planet on. Wow.

If we can believe, in this moment, in the reality of the power of this intimacy for this emergence—in our personal lives, our collective lives, and in the life of this Church—then we can allow God, as the third person, through everyone and through us.

But let's place ourselves in the story now, as the critical element. We are part of the first church in humanity's history to take this on with a full story, through us, and happening now.

I would just like to declare that I can feel in my personal life a new trajectory, and it has to do with joining in intimacy with this Church, with each of you. It is with this collective intimacy, as we get to know each other evermore intimately—which I think is going to be a function of the Church, to deepen the personal intimacy—that we are now declaring to the Universe that a new trajectory is happening right here.

BECOMING GOD'S UNIQUE INTIMACIES

Let's go all the way together in this lifetime. Let's create intimacies. We can step back, we can come closer, but we never look away. We never look away, and we always deepen.

We think that all these public things we do out there are what make the difference. They're important, and we need to make the revolution out there. But the place that it really happens is internally, in the place where I could have contracted, where I could have stepped back. I think that I make the difference because *I'm coaching, I'm teaching, I'm doing something with the President of the United States*, or whatever it is.

You think that's where you make the difference. It's not. It's how we hold the integrity of our intimacies.

We all make mistakes in intimacy. It's about how we fix them, transform them, apologize, step in together, and go deeper. **It's when you don't walk away, and you stay in—in the most personal, intimate circle—you transform it and come together with your beloveds.**

- Your beloved can be your friend.
- Your beloved can be your community.
- Your beloved can be your partner.
- Your beloved can be your teacher.
- Your beloved can be your student.
- Your beloved can be your son, your daughter.

You come together and make it deeper.

Then you reach wider and wider, until we create a Field of Intimacy, which is the Divine Field, and **we each become God's unique intimacies**.

Together, we form an intimate Unique Self Symphony, in which everyone's playing their own instrument and listening deeply to each other.

CHAPTER FIVE

OUR CRISIS IS A BIRTH: ALL CRISIS IS A CRISIS OF INTIMACY

Episode 158 — October 19, 2019

WE LIVE IN AN INTIMATE UNIVERSE

The commitment that Barbara and I made to each other was: *Let's genuinely become a deeper level of what I call whole mate.* Barbara calls it "joining genius," but we're referring to the same thing. We said, *Let's actually become completely egoless.*

All of us in Church, we're completely egoless because we're so blown open with love. It's an actual feeling; I call it "mad love." Rumi talked about it. I don't want to be with anyone who doesn't love madly.

The only thing that heals the personal contraction of the human being— the only thing that loves open the contraction of trauma, the brokenness of being human, of feeling somehow not attuned to, not met, and not seen— **is to love the moment open and to realize that Reality itself is a stage for love.**

The Universe, at its core, is a Love Story: from quarks to atoms, to molecules, cells, and culture.

From quarks to culture, the whole story is a story of allurement.

I'm going to tell you something wild:

Sound, color, physical objects, everything you see, none of it exists as you think it does in the world.

It's a much deeper conversation, but there's a very strong case to be made against reality as we know it. One neuroscientist, Donald Hoffman, points this out in a book called *The Case Against Reality*, which completely aligns with the great traditions. My dear friend, Ervin László, whom Barbara introduced me to, has written extensively about this. The three of us have had many conversations, and we're writing about it in other contexts.

This whole "solid" Reality in front of you? All these atoms?

Atoms are empty; atoms are probability waves of intimacy.

Of course, we have to take physical Reality super seriously because it's the place in which we play. But actually, it's all a stage, and on the stage, we grow open into it, we love open into it, and we release the contractions. **We find each other, we're allured to each other, we join genius, we take responsibility, and we blow Reality open with a level of grace, beauty, goodness, and love.** We realize the potential of Divinity, which is Divinity's greatest yearning. Divinity yearns for intimacy in every moment.

Infinity yearned for intimacy, and Infinity loved finitude, because finitude was a place in which Divinity could manifest this explosion of love and intimacy.

Now, you might ask me: *Why is there all the suffering in the world?*

I don't know. I wrote a long book on it, but I don't know. Suffering is a mystery. But here's the one thing we know. **All suffering means is that there's a failure of intimacy.** You can't even talk about suffering if we don't live in an Intimate Universe because why shouldn't people suffer?

The very fact of suffering *means* that we live in an Intimate Universe: *there shouldn't be suffering.* There is suffering, and it's a failure of intimacy, so we restore intimacy. That's what we mean when we say, *We live in a world of outrageous pain, and the only response is Outrageous Love.*

Pain is outrageous because there's a failure of intimacy. We respond with Outrageous Love by committing Outrageous Acts of Love and restoring intimacy.

This new source code is rooted in the interior and exterior sciences—in the fragrances of physics and in the deepest understandings of all the deepest gnosis from premodern, modern, and postmodern thought, woven into a new story.

That's the new Evolutionary Story.

WE HAVE THE ABILITY TO TELL A NEW STORY: HUMANS ARE LOVERS

The failure of a shared narrative of meaning and nobility, the failure to understand who we fundamentally are, is the source of existential risk (all ten major forms of it) that will take us down in this moment of the sixth mass extinction. Even without existential risk, there's what is called catastrophic risk. (Existential risk means we all go. Catastrophic risk means two or three billion of us go, or suffer unbearably.) With this new story, we can respond to that.

I'm about to burst out crying because it's so important. I just want you to get what this means. We have the ability to tell a new story, just like da Vinci and a thousand other people in the Renaissance told a new story that changed Reality.

But da Vinci's story is no longer enough. It's a story of exteriors, a story of how the scientific structures might create enormous progress in particular domains using the scientific method. But it's not enough. **It's not enough**

of a story of *who the human being is, what our purpose is,* and *what it means that the Universe is a Love Story.*

There was this explosion of imagination through science and exteriors, but we didn't imagine new visions of our identity—based on the deepest sciences, the best neuroscience, and the best psychology. We just didn't do it.

We exploded in exteriors; our imagination literalized as technology. But we didn't literalize our interior imagination and develop the social and spiritual technologies to generate a shared narrative that would bring us together and allow us to create heaven on earth.

As a result, not only do we have dystopian possibilities ahead of us, but we have a current dystopian reality for so many people. A huge amount of the world is suffering. We started with half a billion people 150 years ago, and now we've got almost eight billion people. Of those, how many live beneath the poverty line?

Of the people who are living great middle-class lives, how many are broken? Depression is rising beyond imagination because we haven't provided a story; we haven't shared the good news.

We have to share the good news.
Human beings are lovers, and they
are gorgeous beyond imagination.

But we can't do surface interventions; we have to evolve the source code.

When I first shared with Barbara the word *source code*, and she shared with me her word *Planetary Pentecost*, we were ecstatic. We realized we were talking about the same thing. The source code means there are deep structures—worldviews based on the best sciences—that we live in and that determine our every move.

We have to evolve the source code, so that there's a shared Story in which everyone understands:

- Who am I?
- What is my gift?
- Why am I needed?
- Why was I intended by Cosmos?
- Why am I wildly significant?
- Why is my love God's deepest desire?

If we don't do that, the level of suffering is unbearable. If we do do that, the level of joy is beyond imagination.

We're just beginning. This is a nascent spark. We have to take this revolution into Reality. **We have to experience that we are revolutionaries of love**—not in a New Age way, not in a fundamentalist way—**in the most profound scientific way: interior science and exterior science.**

We get who we are, and we're willing to be that, manifest that, incarnate that, and love it open.

- We want to alleviate suffering.
- We want to heal the pain.
- We want to bring the separate parts together.
- We want to activate social synergy. That is completely possible, and it depends on each one of us stepping forward, in the thousand ways we can make this real.

Are we ready to play a larger game? YES! That's the holy YES. That's the YES of the Big Bang.

PRAYER: EXPONENTIALIZING THE PASSION AND TENDERNESS OF OUR MOST INTIMATE EXPERIENCE

We're about to enter into prayer. Let's find the inside place of prayer. Let's literally do this together, and let's make these words *our* words.

So what is prayer? **Prayer is when we turn to God, who's not only the Infinity of Power but the Infinity of Intimacy.**

Now, let's make it real. What does the Infinity of Intimacy mean?

Imagine your most intimate moment—your most tender moment and your most passionate moment—because intimacy can be tender, and intimacy can be passionate. Deeply feel that moment—and then double it, triple it, quadruple it.

Feel it inside. Access the moment. Take your time.

Hold it for a second. Find the moment. It might be a moment of tenderness with a child or with a friend. It might be a moment of passion and tenderness with a beloved. Take the passion and tenderness and bring them together. Find that beloved. Locate that moment. Now double the moment, triple the moment, quadruple the moment, times ten, times 100, times 1,000.

Now you can feel dripping, pulsing, tender, and quivering intimacy moving through you beyond imagination. You're about to burst until your physical body can't hold you, and you become quivering tenderness, radically alive, wild, holy, ecstatic passion. *You are passion itself.* Imagine the deepest pleasure you've ever experienced in your life and exponentialize it—you're melting into a level of pleasure that's utterly unimaginable. **That's a fraction of the experience of the Infinity of Intimacy, looking at you and desiring you.**

God is the force of Cosmos—God inheres in the four forces: the strong and the weak nuclear, the electromagnetic, and the gravitational—**but all those forces *inhere* with Eros, and Eros is the movement of Reality towards ever deeper intimacy.**

The quality of Eros is desire. Reality, God, desires more intimacy. That Godforce, that Spark, the quality of Eros that lives in us, desires deeper and deeper intimacy.

Every crisis along the way is a crisis of intimacy, and the crisis then generates more intimacy.

PRAYER: LOVING AND BEING LOVED MADLY

When we turn to God, we're turning to the Infinity of Intimacy that hears us speaking. I can hear you speaking because I'm intelligent. But my intelligence is part of the Field of LoveIntelligence. My intelligence is part of the Field of LoveDesire. It's part of the Field of LoveBeauty. So just as I can hear you talking, the Field of Intelligence hears you talking.

Every word we say is heard; there's no extra word. **If you awaken to Reality, you feel, as Rumi felt, the Beloved whispering in my ear every moment:** *I love you madly. I desire you madly. I love you so much.*

That's not metaphor. That's real.

Love is not hard to find—love is impossible to avoid. Reality is desiring you, intending you, choosing you, recognizing you, holding you, loving, and adoring you in every second.

We turn to God, who's the Infinity of Intimacy. That's a realization of enlightenment. We call that God in the second person.

God in the first person is God who lives in me.

God in the third person is the force of Cosmos.

God in the second person is the Infinity of Intimacy that passionately desires me, that quiveringly holds me in every second and whispers in my ear: *I need you. Let's do this together. Let's create Reality together. Let's create heaven on earth. I've created this illusion for you. Take it seriously, the physical world, but it's just a stage. Will you do it with Me?*

Here's the prerequisite, says God: You have to love me madly, and I've got to love you madly, and we've got to love each other madly. But mad means what's true on the inside.

So bring me everything you have. Bring me your holy and your broken Hallelujah. Bring me every yearning and I'm going to hold it with you. I'm going to honor it, and I'm going to kiss it open. Then, when you feel so totally received and held, we're going to turn together towards the world as evolution awake in us, evolution as love in action, and we're going to love Reality open in a way that's never been done before.

That's the truth.

So please, says the divine voice, says the Infinity of Intimacy: *Will you bring me your holy and broken Hallelujah? Will you bring me everything?*

Hallelujah! We turn to the Infinity of Intimacy and ask for everything. So I invite every prayer, She invites every prayer, and we invite any and every prayer. When we pray, we realize that every word is heard and matters madly—and we ask for everything.

Because prayer affirms the dignity of personal need.

EVOLUTIONARY LOVE CODE: ENLIGHTENMENT MEANS INTIMACY WITH ALL PERSONS AND THINGS

Our crisis is a birth, personally and collectively, because crisis is an evolutionary driver.

Every great crisis at its root is a crisis in intimacy.

Crisis means that someone or something is being left out of the circle.

Enlightenment means intimacy with all persons and things.

Enlightenment means that there are no externalities.

The solution to every great crisis is a new and deeper configuration of intimacy.

Reality is moving towards more intimacy; God desires more intimacy. It means there's no one left out of the circle. There are no "deplorables." But it also means that *there's no part of us that's left out of the circle; there's no part of my story that's cut off; there's no part of me that's split away.*

When I'm not inside, and I'm not feeling the Eros of Reality uniquely configured, and I don't realize that *I'm a unique configuration of intimacy and desire that's needed by All-That-Is*, then I don't realize *I'm already in the circle*. Every time I feel excluded, I'm devastated—when I'm actually already in the circle. But when I don't *experience* myself as being in the circle, the way I find my way is: I place other people outside the circle.

By placing other people outside the circle, I give myself the illusion of being on the inside. That's not a casual sentence, that is the fucking structure of our society!

Our society is built on a win/lose metrics—the entire thing, all the way up and all the way down. Every department of government, business, and relationship has some dimension of power struggle, a win/lose metrics, meaning, *I win if you lose.* And therefore, that win/lose metrics generates a story. It's called a success story: *I succeed only if you lose.* There's no sense of *we succeed together.* There's no sense that the separate self is an illusion; separation is an illusion.

The desire of Reality has been, from the very beginning, to bring quarks, atoms, and molecules together to create new wholes. **The desire for intimacy is a new shared identity in which we're together. We individuate, and we're gorgeously unique. But we're unique expressions of this organismic explosion of Outrageous Love creating heaven on earth.** That's not a success story. That's not a win/lose metrics. That's the movement towards a new evolutionary intimacy. That's a planetary awakening in love through Unique Self Symphonies.

Now, **if I leave part of myself out**—if I leave part of myself in the trauma and in the limiting belief, I split off that part of me which was too painful, if I'm afraid to go all the way in this lifetime—**then I'm not accessing my unique voice**.

I can only find my unique voice and speak my prophecy, if all of me is included, if I haven't ripped out pages from my Book of Life. It has to be all inside of me. It all has to be part of my story.

Every detour is a destination. Every rogue path is part of my rapture. We have to find our way, to bring it all together. It's the holy and the broken *Hallelujah* where nothing is split off. The crisis in my life is a crisis of intimacy with myself.

I can't be a prophet, I can't speak my prophecy, unless I'm intimate with *every single part of myself* and I integrate the whole thing—and then I blow it open and love it open.

CHAPTER SIX

ENLIGHTENMENT IS INTIMACY WITH ALL PEOPLE AND ALL THINGS

Episode 159 — October 26, 2019

IF IT'S YOUR LAST BREATH, MY LOVE, THEN IT'S MY LAST BREATH TOO

I read a text yesterday, and I have to not cry when I say this. They found a truck with thirty-nine bodies, and the bodies were of girls who were being transported. They were trying to get out of their country and get to freedom. But there was no air. So the girl texts her mother and she says: *I can't breathe. Our dream of freedom isn't going to happen. I'm sorry. I love you.*

That should never happen.

No girl should ever be out of breath. No one should be suffocated. Because there's enough food in our world to feed everyone four times over, and there's enough air for all of us to breathe into each other.

As we were here in Church, as people were out seeing a movie, maybe eating a doughnut, she was breathing her last breath.

She is us, and we are her.

*I commit my last breath, and we
commit our last breath together,
to bring down the source code and
deliver it into the fabric of Reality.*

We now understand that the world is not made up of separate parts. Newtonian/Cartesian science, which was so critical in the Renaissance and took us forward, is currently insufficient. We now understand that actually *there are no separate things.*

- That an atom itself is a probability wave of relationship.
- That the Universe is, in our language, a Love Story.
- That we live in a CosmoErotic Universe all the way up and all the way down.
- That we breathe into each other literally; we literally breathe into each other.

The crisis is based in the old win/lose metrics, where *you're either number one or number two.* That's not the case. **In Hebrew, the word *echad* one doesn't mean one as a number one. It means one as in *yichud*: you're unique, you're singular.**

Every crisis is a crisis of intimacy. We feel like we're going to be intimate if we're with the one, and we're the one, and the one means we're number one, and *we're going to make America great again.* It's a *rivalrous America that's going to be great, and we're going to fight everyone else.* No, that's not how we trump in Reality.

I remember I was with Ram Dass, my dear friend, and we were in Maui a bunch of years ago, when George Bush was President. He had George Bush on his altar. He says, *I'm going to love George Bush because he's yearning also.* So Donald Trump is on my altar. I think we need to do everything we can to remove him from office—not to degrade him, not to demean him, just to remove him from office—because that's part of the constitutional process.

And I also feel the brokenness of his heart, and I feel the yearning, and I feel the emptiness of *only if I'm number one do I exist.* **No, it's not about being number one. It's about understanding that** *I'm the unique one; I'm the singular one.*

The crisis of intimacy is solved when we begin to understand that there's a planetary awakening in love through Unique Self Symphonies, where each of us plays our own irreducibly unique and gorgeous instrument of Evolutionary Love, giving our unique gifts, singing our unique songs, writing our unique poems, and being the dazzling light that only you and only I can be.

I get to celebrate you, and you get to celebrate me.

That's what it means. When there's a crisis of intimacy, when there's a crisis of Eros, it means we need to create new structures of intimacy and Eros. That's what this church is: One Church. When we say One Church, we immediately say: One Church, Many Paths; each path is unique, beautiful, and gorgeous. It's One Mountain—we're all playing the same music; Many Paths—there are many gorgeous instruments in the symphony.

If you can't breathe, my love—if you're eleven years old, you can't breathe, and you're texting your mother because you can't breathe—**and it's your last breath, then it's my last breath.**

We have to know that in our bodies.

It's one world. It's One Heart. It's One Church. It's One Nation. It's One Love. That's the evolution of love. That's the crisis of intimacy that we need to move beyond.

Are we ready to play a larger game, a true game of One Love and One Heart?

Are we ready to participate and to be the evolution of love?

Are we ready to be a new configuration of intimacy, where it's not about one as in number one, but where we're all singular, unique, and all number one together in some way?

We have all of our unique relationships with each other that are different, and we get to be unique and singular. Oh my God, we can do this all the way!

EVOLUTIONARY LOVE CODE: EVERY CRISIS AT ITS ROOT IS A CRISIS OF INTIMACY

Our crisis is a birth, personally and collectively, because crisis is an evolutionary driver.

Every great crisis at its root is a crisis in intimacy.

Crisis means that someone or something is being left out of the circle.

Enlightenment means intimacy with all persons and things.

Enlightenment means that there are no externalities.

The solution to every great crisis is a new and deeper configuration of intimacy.

We turn to God. We understand that God is not only the Infinity of Power. God is not only the Divinity that lives in us, as us, and through us. God is the Infinity of Intimacy that uniquely configures as us. God is the Infinity of Intimacy that holds us. As Rumi says, *I want to fall into the arms of the Beloved*, meaning, God is not only the Infinity of Intimacy in us, but the Infinity of Intimacy who holds us, whom we turn to, who knows our name, and who holds our holy and our broken *Hallelujah*.

When we pray, we participate in the evolution of prayer itself. Prayer is not turning to the cosmic vending machine in the sky, owned by one religion who says *it's my God, it's my love, and my love means only me and my people.* No, God is not the god who is commodified and sold back to us. God is the Infinity of Intimacy that says *my Marc*—and that "my" includes all of us.

God literally holds each of us individually and knows each of our names.

We come to God and we say: *Oh my God, Infinity of Intimacy*—like Rumi to the Beloved—we ask for everything.

We ask for our personal needs because prayer affirms the dignity of personal need.

We ask beyond our personal need because we understand that *her breath is our breath, and that no one's ultimately separate.*

It's all a love story. We're interconnected and need each other desperately. Because *to say I love you is to say I need you.*

Let's take these prayers and literally lift them to the sky. Let's blow them out to the sky. Let's blow it open like we've never loved it open in the world. Every time we pray, we love it open. We pray to the Goddess who holds us. We commit to this moment as if this gathering were our last, as if it were our last moment, as if this were our last breath.

What do we say in our last breath? What did that beautiful girl say? She's now in her continuity of consciousness. She said, *I love you.* So we now say *I love you* to each other, and we love this moment open. We expand our circle. **Every person who's been outside of our circle, and every part who's not been connected, everything that's been in some sort of ultimate separation, and every split-off part of ourselves—we bring it all together, raise it up, intertwine it in love, and love this moment open.**

We want to pour resources into the heart of the source code of Reality itself, using all the modes of communication, to take this new story, to take this da Vinci moment, and love Reality open at this moment between dystopia and utopia.

So never again will there be a child out of breath, suffocating because they're being transported to freedom by an abusive commodifying merchant who forgot that they were human beings.

It's not just that one child; *that one child is exponentialized all over the world.*

We're in a moment where our crisis could be a birth. Our crisis could evolve us to literally create heaven on earth. Politics and love need to come together. We're creating a politics of love. We're beyond church and state, but politics and religion do need to come together. Religion comes from *re-ligare*: we're reconnected, and no one's left out.

Our crisis is a birth. Every crisis is a crisis of intimacy, a crisis of Eros. We need to find deeper and new ways to love each other.

It means new models of relationship that transcend and include the best of the old models.

It means relationship that is not based on win/lose metrics, where I'm in because everybody else is out. No, that means *I'm not really in the circle; I'm only in because everyone else is out*, that's my illusion of being in. We need to remember: *I'm in because I'm in, not because you're out.*

Every country plays an instrument in the Unique Self Symphony.

Every religion plays an instrument in the Unique Self Symphony.

Everyone is uniquely, gorgeously needed.

Reality needs your service.

CHAPTER SEVEN

MY CRISIS IS MY BIRTH—
REALITY DESIRES MY BIRTH

Episode 160 — November 2, 2019

MIRARI: STANDING IN RAPT ATTENTION BEFORE THE MIRACLE

There's a beautiful old saying, in the words of my teachers. They said it in Yiddish, so I'll translate it loosely into English: *The master can make the miracle happen, but if no one tells the story of the miracle, then it didn't happen.*

In some sense, Divinity, God, the Infinity of Intimacy, made this Story. It's our job to tell the Story. It's a Story of a miracle. A miracle means, originally in Latin, *mirari*. It means *to behold with rapt attention*. It's to allow yourself to feel the rapture of Reality.

You can look at biochemistry, talk about the folding of proteins, and forget what a protein is. A protein is a string of amino acids. What's an amino acid? **An amino acid is a configuration of allurement in which individuated particles, which are individuated expressions of the Infinity of Intimacy, seek each other, blown open by Eros, coming together in a dazzling configuration and symphony of intimacy in order to create life.**

We call that a chemical reaction, and we dismiss it. Because language reveals and language also hides.

We have to stand *mirari*, naked before the miracle, with rapt attention and know that it's a very particular kind of miracle that defines our Reality. This is the essence of the whole Story: **it's a miracle that demands our partnership, a miracle that demands we co-create with it.** The intention of Cosmos is clear: for human beings to awaken with the rest of all Reality.

Human beings are the expression—the co-creative, conscious expression that we're aware of in ourselves, which has:

- ♦ The capacity to build hospitals,
- ♦ The capacity to breathe life into every child,
- ♦ The capacity to hold all who are broken and dispossessed,
- ♦ The capacity to heal disease,
- ♦ The capacity to hold a baby and to feed a baby.
- ♦ **All of evolution is conscious. All of evolution is intelligent. But evolution is awakening uniquely in us at this critical juncture in history and is saying to us:** *I need you. Be my partner. Make the miracle with me. Tell the story of the miracle. Be the miracle.*

At this moment in history, it's telling the story of the miracle. It's about bringing together the best wisdom of all the traditions with the leading-edge understandings of science in all of its realms, the social sciences and the physical sciences, to weave together a new story. We weave all this into a systemic source code change that allows us to move from devolution to evolution, allowing us to move from a potential dystopia, which is literally at the door, to a utopia—at this moment in the world, in this moment right now.

As we are gathered here at this Church, there are at least two billion people intensely suffering from physical deprivation. But I'll tell you something else. There are another five billion people who are desperately looking for joy. There are seven billion people on this planet, and every single one of them is looking for joy.

Every one of us is asking: *How do I transform my life? How do I turn my life into a triumph?*

There's a word in Hebrew, *olam*, which means "the world," and it also means "hidden"—the hidden structure of the world. **The world is structured as a secret garden; you have to find your way in; you have to journey.**

The way we become realized as human beings is that we have to find and reveal the miracle; we have to find our way.

That's the structure of Reality: we're born as an expression of the great Glory, the great One, the great Beauty. Then we fall away. We don't literally fall away, but we fall asleep.

It's not a mistake or some accident. The fall from Eden isn't a glitch in the system. No, it's part of the intention.

- I've got to find my way out of the matrix.
- I've got to wake up.
- I've got to claim my joy.
- I've got to claim my beauty.
- I've got to claim the miracle.
- I've got to become the miracle.

And it's not always obvious.

WE'RE HERE TO TELL AND TO BE THE NEW UNIVERSE STORY

There are seven billion people on this planet right now, and every single one of them is looking for a way to turn their lives into a triumph. The only way that can happen is if we have a shared sense of Reality: If we have a Story, a shared Story, which tells us something about who we are. From that place, we find the way to individuate Divinity in every single one of us, in this gorgeous-beyond-imagination Unique Self Symphony, which has such unimaginable joy, such unimaginable rapture, such unimaginable goodness.

We have to model it. We have to start it. We have to do it. We have to find a place where we can tell that Story.

- We're here to tell the Story.
- We're here to be da Vinci in this generation.
- We're here as a band of Outrageous Lovers, to be the Christ, to be the Abraham, to be the Muhammad.
- We're here to *be* the change the world desperately needs.
- We're here, we are excited, and we are alive.
- We're going to make mistakes, but we're going to make mistakes in the right direction.
- We're coming together.
- We are the planetary awakening in love through Unique Self Symphonies.

Friends, what's our intention? Our intention is to play a larger game. So just one question for you: *Are we ready to play a larger game?*

- We're ready to play a larger game.
- We're ready to be the love that the world needs.
- We're ready to untie all the knots in our personal lives, be open as love, and literally change the world—because that's what the world desperately wants us to do in this very second.

ITS INSIDES ARE LINED WITH LOVE

I want to show you a couple of books: my book called *Radical Kabbalah*, and Barbara's book, *Evolutionary Testament*. We're going to talk about these two books because one of the things we want to do is to weave the old lineages together with the new sciences and synergize them. Synergy

71

means *creating a whole that's greater than the sum of its parts*. We are weaving together the new story.

There's a very beautiful and ancient teaching of the lineages that is now becoming apparent. It's the core of what we're saying when we talk about a planetary awakening in love through Unique Self Symphonies. The teaching was written by King Solomon. Have you heard of any other ancient Near Eastern kings? Well, the reason you haven't is because Solomon was doing something special. Solomon and Hammurabi were the two really important figures then.

Solomon was saying something very important. He understood something. He opened up the Eye of the Spirit, the eye of the interior sciences. **He intuited and understood something crucial about the very nature of Reality, and he said it in three words.** *Tocho ratzuf ahava: its insides are lined with love.*

That's what *Radical Kabbalah* is all about. It's about this lineage that talks about *its insides are lined with love*, which means that love is not outside of Reality. It's not "there's a God outside, up there loving us unworthy humans here." No, *tocho*: its insides, the very inside, the very fabric of Reality is a Love Story.

The fabric of Reality is *Amor*.

There's a realization that *Homo sapiens* has to go to the next stage, that the wisdom of *Homo sapiens* has taken us so far and now we need to jump to a higher level of realization to integrate and synergize everything we've learned and bring it all together. This is the emergence of *Homo amor*, the New human and the new humanity. There have been lots of names in the last fifty years: the gnostic human, the ultra-human, the continuous human—Barbara will talk a little bit about those today.

The core that we understand is that *its insides are lined with love*.

- Reality is not a fact.
- Reality is a story.

- ◆ It's not an ordinary story.
- ◆ It's a love story.
- ◆ It's not an ordinary love story—*its insides are lined with love.*
- ◆ It's an Evolutionary Love Story. It's an Outrageous Love Story.

Who am I? *I'm a unique expression of that Outrageous Love.*

Love is at the center; let's access that truth of Reality. Why do we like love songs so much?

Why is love so central in your life? Not because you're aberrant, but because that's the truth of Reality: *its insides are lined with love.*

PRAYER: WE'RE INDIVIDUATED EXPRESSIONS OF— AND HELD BY—THE ALL-THAT-IS

What's prayer? God is not only the Infinity of Power; God is the Infinity of Intimacy.

Intimacy means that we have a shared identity. It means, *I'm coming closer, and that I realize we're not ultimately separate. Even though we're individuated, we're higher individuations beyond ego; we're individuated expressions of the LoveDesire and LoveBeauty and LoveIntelligence.*

Yet, we're held by All-That-Is. So in prayer, we turn to All-That-Is, we turn to the God who knows our name, we turn to the Infinity of Intimacy and we say: *Oh my God, give me everything.* But not a selfish everything, not a self everything:

- ◆ Give me everything I need to be in radical joy and to share joy.
- ◆ Give me everything I need as a Unique Self in my unique circle of intimacy and influence.
- ◆ Give me everything I need to be so alive and radiant that I can take responsibility as Your partner and co-creator.

We ask for health, means, and ease. We ask for everyone around us. **We pray for ourselves because prayer affirms the dignity of personal need, and then we pray for the world.**

I just want you to know that prayer moves the world. Our colleague Larry Dossey has written a great book on prayer. At the moment, about two-thirds of the medical schools in the country are beginning to have courses on the role of prayer. This wasn't true thirty years ago. *What does prayer have to do with anything?*

There's a realization that turning towards others with radical love and compassion has an impact. Prayer is real. Prayer is part of the fabric of Cosmos.

The space-time continuum in which we live, the physical material world, is an expression of an underlying Field of Consciousness. **The underlying Field of Consciousness is love itself; it is Eros. This means that when I pray from a place of radical love, I can impact what is happening structurally in the space-time continuum.**

We should do all the medicine in the world. All of the structure of medicine that needs to happen in the world needs to happen; it's a holy expression of the Divine. Together, integrated with that—because it's all part of the same fabric; it's all part of the same One—is: *we pray. We love each other madly when we're sick. We hold each other. We love each other open, which is the beginning of all healing.*

We turn to God, the Infinity of Intimacy, and pray for ourselves.

We pray for each other.

We pray for the world.

THE EVOLUTIONARY TESTAMENT OF CREATION: THE PROMISE WILL BE KEPT

In this moment, I am honoring the Church of Evolutionary Love. I'm placing this Church in the context of the evolution of humanity. I'm going back to the roots of this Church, reconnecting with our roots. Like Marc is saying, let's connect with the existing political Reality and put our love into it wherever we put it. So I am now today going back to our roots, to the New Testament, and I want to read you one or two things that Jesus said.

But before I do, I'll just give this slight little background, so we can see how the New Testament is the future that we're already bringing through in the new Church as it comes from our roots. As you know, I come from a Jewish, agnostic, secular, materialistic, and militaristic family. I actually got the perfect start, like being ejected out of a cannon.

There's a really great sequence here, beginning with **Maslow**. He studied wellness rather than sickness, and he had the image of a self-actualizing person who has found chosen work intrinsically self-rewarding. So, I became a student of Maslow.

The next one was **Teilhard de Chardin**, a Catholic scientist who had barely published in his lifetime. Basically, what he saw was that Jesus was the future human, the ultra-human. He saw that the entire direction of evolution— from single-celled to multi-celled, to animals, to humans—was leading towards what he called the "ultra-human," or the Christ. **Sri Aurobindo** called it the "gnostic human." **Buckminster Fuller** called it the "continuous human." So all my future-oriented guides were able to offer this.

Then, I met some Catholic Sisters—and I want you to know, they're running the church. They are absolutely great, and they almost made me into a Catholic sister. They kept asking me, "When did you become a Catholic, Barbara?" I said, "Well, I'm not actually a Catholic." They said, "Well, you certainly sound like one."

Because they had been deeply influenced by **Brian Swimme** and by the evolutionary philosophy of Teilhard de Chardin and other great thinkers, they invited me to speak before all the Catholic women of the world who were running the church. I spoke about conscious evolution.

I have to tell you this: An article was written in a key Catholic newspaper that some woman had come to speak at the Catholic Sisters global convention, and this woman dared to talk about "conscious evolution." The Vatican was afraid that it would destroy the faith of the Catholic Sisters. So, along with the feminists who were also in trouble, I was heavily criticized. The worst of all was a woman who was a conscious evolutionary.

So amidst all of that, one day, while taking a walk, I saw the huge Statue of the Resurrection there in the Garden at Santa Barbara. The inner voice said: *Barbara, when you love God above all else, when you love your neighbor as yourself, and when you love yourself as a natural Christ, combined with science and technology, you will all be changed. I want demonstrations now. Barbara, I want you to be a demonstration of the love of God, of nature, of self, as a natural Christ, aided and abetted by science and technology, giving us powers of Gods.*

The awesome Reality is that's exactly what's coming. But we're not bringing our holy texts forward, and we're certainly not putting God into high technology with Evolutionary Love. So I'm setting out a huge path here for the Evolutionary Church, which is to **go back to the ancient texts and the history they've created on this earth and then jump forward into the very growing edge of our culture.** Let's bring this in, and let's reunite all those other churches who believe in this. Let's invite them to join us in seeing what's becoming. This is a huge thing!

So I said to Marc, would you mind if today I read two small gospels out of *The Evolutionary Testament of Co-Creation*? This is a published volume that anybody can have, *The Evolutionary Testament of Co-Creation: The Promise Will Be Kept.*

I thought I would just do something very simple to get started here. I've invited Marc to join me in teaching both the Kabbalah and the Evolutionary Testament from the point of view of its evolutionary implications. If Marc and I do that, I tell you, this is going to be holy.

So here you are, beloved. This is Matthew 1, from The Gospel According to Matthew:

> In those days came John the Baptist, preaching in the wilderness of Judaea and saying, Repent ye: for the kingdom of heaven is at hand. For this is who that was spoken of by the prophet Esaias, saying, *The voice of one crying in the wilderness, Prepare ye the way of the Lord, make his paths straight.*

This is my interpretation. Intuition lives deep in the memory of humankind, informing us that we are more than animals destined to repeat the endless mammalian cycle of eating, sleeping, reproducing, and dying. That's the mammalian cycle.

The words of John the Baptist reveal to us that we are unfinished. He was absolutely right. **Something more awaits us: a release of our potential, a fulfillment of our aspirations.** Repent, John said, for the kingdom of heaven is at hand. Repent means to change our minds, to be dissatisfied with our present, incomplete condition, knowing that within us is a state of being much greater than we've yet realized. **We are the kingdom of heaven when our full potential is realized.**

- ◆ So repent, transform, and align with God.
- ◆ Do not accept your present limits.
- ◆ The time for newness is at hand.

Now here is Matthew 3:9 and 3:10:

> And think not to say within yourselves, We have Abraham to our father: for I say unto you, that God is able of these stones to raise up children unto Abraham. And now also the axe is laid unto the root of the trees: therefore, every tree which bringeth

not forth good fruit is hewn down and cast into the fire.

This is what John was doing. John the Baptist, who prepared the way for Jesus, told the Jews, the sons of Abraham, that they would be known by their acts, not by their lineage. Any act that does not serve the good will be unable to take root and thrive in the new world; only the good will endure. It does not matter where we come from or where our parents are. It matters only who we are, where we are going, and whether or not we will deliver our highest potential. So this goes on and on.

I'll just read you this: *Then comes Jesus from Galilee.* Just try to imagine that world, with somebody preparing a way for the new human that we find ourselves just now becoming, and that new human appears as Jesus.

> Then cometh Jesus from Galilee to Jordan unto John, to be baptized of him. But John forbad him, saying, I have need to be baptized of you, and come you to me? And Jesus answered, said unto him, *Suffer it to be so now: for thus it becomes us to fulfill all righteousness.*

Let's realize that what we have here is the root of Western culture, and to some degree, of all world-oriented evolutionary culture: a being who came in and manifested what we are becoming.

I was really astonished, and because I was a friend of Jonas Salk when I was reading this, I went to the monastery and checked in there, and I kept writing paragraph after paragraph. Jonas was taking me to these laboratories where they had stamped out physical death. Then I'd read in the New Testament, Jesus said: *Lazarus, arise! And Lazarus arose. And you shall not die.*

So I thought, you know what, folks? **Western culture, and modern culture in general, is developing the capacity to act out the vision of life ever-evolving.** Our New Testament was the first enormous writing from this person who knew all this.

There's this other book of mine, which is really so incredible, called *The Revelation*. I'll just read you this last little piece from Corinthians 15:52. St. Paul wrote:

> Behold, I show you a mystery: we shall not all sleep, but we shall all be changed. In a moment, in the twinkling of an eye, at the last trump: for the trumpet shall sound, and the dead shall be raised incorruptible, and we shall all be changed.

So I'd like to just conclude this by saying, is it possible that the Church of Evolutionary Love is actually the site for the church of the evolving human? That by bringing these ancient texts, as well as the highest degree of technology into our church, we will set a template for the future of humanity as an Evolutionary Church. I ask you that question.

EVOLUTIONARY LOVE CODE: EVERY CRISIS IS A BIRTH

> Our crisis is a birth, personally and collectively, because crisis is an evolutionary driver.
>
> Every great crisis at its root is a crisis in intimacy.
>
> Crisis means that someone or something is being left out of the circle.
>
> Enlightenment means intimacy with all persons and things. Enlightenment means that there are no externalities.
>
> The solution to every great crisis is a new and deeper configuration of intimacy.

Our crisis is a birth, personally and collectively, because crisis is an evolutionary driver. What does that mean? Let's just find this together; we've got to make this real. Every single one of us has engaged in crisis:

- ◆ It can be a crisis of health,
- ◆ It can be a crisis of a broken heart,

- ◆ It can be a crisis of enduring false accusation,
- ◆ It can be a crisis of injustice,
- ◆ It can be a crisis of opportunity that you deserve that didn't come to you,
- ◆ It can be a crisis of being misrecognized.

A crisis means you want to break. The Hebrew word for crisis is *shever*: the broken, breaking. *The holy and the broken Hallelujah.* The broken *Hallelujah* is about the crisis.

And even though it all went wrong.

It all went wrong is about the crisis.

She tied you to a kitchen chair. She broke your throne, and she cut your hair. It's about the crisis. But our crisis is a birth. To know that every time I break down, there's an opening that I can break through. There's a beautiful sacred text which says:

Ve'hayu ha'devarim ha'eileh, asher Anochi me'tzav'cha hayom al levavecha, "The words that I share with you today in my deepest intimacy should be on your heart."

Why are the words *on* your heart? Shouldn't the words be *in* your heart? So the masters say: **Only when your heart breaks—only when there's a crisis and your heart opens— can the words drop in.**

Our crisis is a birth. Three years ago, I went through an enormously hard period of time, which almost paralyzed my heart. In a particular vector of suffering, it was pretty much as high as you can go. What did I do? In this time of immense pain, I went inside. And I sat with Kristina, and together we wrote *A Return to Eros.*

It was a time of a failure of Eros. So we took all of the crisis and turned it into a birth.

Every single one of us can do that. This is the best book on Eros and the CosmoErotic Universe in the world today, and I say that unabashedly. Not with egoic pride, but with divine pride and delight. Thank you, Goddess, that we are able to articulate this vision.

This is true about every single one of us. Your crisis and my crisis is a birth.

I want to ask you if you are willing to write *"My crisis is a birth."* It's not abstract.

Let's take the next step. My crisis is *my* birth, not *a* birth. I'm going to ask you if you're willing to go the next step, but you have to actually feel it in your body.

- ◆ My birth is needed by God.
- ◆ My birth is not a detail.
- ◆ My birth is not some little personal development moment.
- ◆ My birth is needed by God.

My birth is intended by God, literally.

Then I have this realization of the deep truth, which is literally:

I am God's partner and lover.

That's who I actually am. That's my actual identity.

I don't have the time to do the physics now. I spent most of last night reading physics. But right now, just to get it:

I am God's partner and lover.

That is the truth of my identity. It's what it means to be an Outrageous Lover.

I am literally God's partner and lover.

Do you know what love is?

- ◆ **Love is the realization that I'm loved madly by All-That-**

Is, I'm needed by All-That-Is, and that I am literally God's partner and lover.

- We're here to tell this new story.
- We're here to be da Vinci together.
- We're here to be audacious.
- We're imperfect, so if I do something wrong, forgive me. If you think I was off about something, you're right, and let it go. It doesn't matter.
- We're going to make mistakes, but we're going to make mistakes in the right direction.
- We're going to do this. This is ours to do.
- We're the band of Outrageous Lovers in this generation.

CHAPTER EIGHT

INCLUDING AND TRANSCENDING: FROM BIOLOGICAL FAMILY TO EVOLUTIONARY FAMILY

Episode 220 — December 27, 2020

BIOLOGICAL FAMILY AND EVOLUTIONARY FAMILY

Biological family is wondrous, and we are committed to it. Evolutionary family, or soul root family, is no less significant and sometimes even more so. At the very least, we need to be as committed to evolutionary family as we are to our biological family, and often much more so.

It is before your evolutionary family that you can confess your greatness, take your unique risk, speak and live your deepest heart's desire, and be seen in the depth of your true glory.

We will not be able to respond to existential risk without making the momentous leap from only our biological family to our evolutionary and soul root family.

Moreover, we're not going to be able to respond to existential risk without honoring and deepening our love of biological family and then opening our hearts and loving just as much, sometimes wildly, our evolutionary family, our soul root family.

THE IMPORTANCE OF BIOLOGICAL FAMILY

Biological family is really important. We were born with our biological family because the intelligence of Cosmos chose that family. It required generations and generations of unique allurements to come together and to be able to choose each other to ultimately generate the family that generated me.

Claud Lelouch did a fantastic movie about this couple that meets each other, and he goes through all the previous generations, so you realize what it took for this couple to meet each other, the webs and webs of allurement that brought people together. *Wow!* How did Petris come together with Veronica? That took everything. It wasn't just Petris and Veronica. It was generations and generations of allurement before them.

We begin to realize that our families are not an accident. There's work to do with our families. There are unique fixings to do with our families.

WE ARE NOT DEFINED BY OUR BIOLOGY

At the same time, one of the things that we're understanding so profoundly— and that the ancients at their best understood but then it got lost—is that evolution is not a straight line. Often, ideas appear and then they get lost. Gorgeous ideas appear sometimes in ancient civilizations, and then they're lost, and then we find them again. Evolution is not a straight line. People were once aware of the idea I'm about to share with you, but it got lost, and it's only now coming back online.

This is the notion that *we're not defined by our biology.*

For example, **we can move beyond**—and this is very complex and misapplied in so many ways—**my narrow identity of man and woman**—*I'm man, but I embrace my she that also lives in me; I am woman, but I embrace my he that also lives in me*—**beyond the clear, biological distinctions that live in the**

man and woman's body. There are a number of very clear hormonal and structural distinctions, but actually, *biology is not destiny.*

However, we do not leave biology behind. This is really critical. It's a very big deal. We don't deny the core essence of how and where we were born.

For most people in the world, you were born a man or a woman. That's a big deal that Reality made that choice, not for everyone, but for the overwhelming majority of people, that's clearly the case.

Even though this is a big deal, nobody is limited by biology. **We don't leave behind biology; we transcend and include biology.** We call that Unique Gender. *I embrace my unique qualities of masculine and feminine, or what we call line and circle.* These are original qualities of Cosmos that live in me. That's my Unique Gender.

The same thing is true about biological family. We don't leave biological family behind. **We're madly committed to our biological family, but that's not the whole story. We transcend and include biology.** I've got a larger family. The larger family are the people that I meet along the way. The people we meet along the way matter.

I want to tell you, if I can, a personal story. In 2006, I suffered an enormous tragedy. I was wrongly attacked, and my biological family didn't question the attack. They were deep in Orthodox Judaism and other forms of Judaism. They thought I was not faithful to Orthodox Judaism, although in my deepest heart, I am: I practice in my own internal, private practice. I put on phylacteries every day, I do Sabbath, I keep kosher. But I was moving beyond Orthodoxy, and in many senses beyond Judaism by practicing the best understandings of Christianity, Buddhism, and Kashmir Shaivism.

When I got falsely attacked, my family disappeared. They didn't call. They assumed that the claims were correct, which they weren't, and so my family was gone. The people who were closest to me were my evolutionary family, who are wonderful teachers, professors, feminists, men's rights activists, people in psychology and politics, and leading abuse-victim advocates.

Those people gathered around me, these fabulous human beings of unimpeachable integrity, were my family.

They were my evolutionary family.

They were my soul root family.

THE IMPORTANCE OF EVOLUTIONARY FAMILY

My soul root family, my evolutionary family—*those are the people I evolve with*. I've got to be radically committed to them in the same way as, and sometimes even more than I'm committed to my biological family.

I want to tell you something shocking, and this is hard to get. There's a great Hasidic master who wrote when he was on his deathbed, and I want you to feel this with me, *I have just one sin that I want to atone for. I want to atone for the sin of loving my son more than the neighbor's boy.*

Now, I'm not saying that you shouldn't love your son more. I'm saying that I get what that master was saying. Do you get the dialectic of that? We've got to take our evolutionary family seriously. We've got to be committed to them.

I'm going to share with you another thing—this is a personal day, a holy day, and a celebration. I want to share that I've personally given away hundreds of thousands of dollars of the little money I have in the world to people in my soul root family, not biological family, because I'm committed to them.

It's always measured in terms of money. What we do is we spend money only on our biological family, and to our soul root family, our evolutionary family, *we write them a nice note*. No. You've got to be committed all the way. Obviously in the best way you can, and obviously we all have to balance our competing concerns and commitments.

I'll just tell you one thing. If you've got $10 million to spend, and you're spending $9 million of it on your biological family and $100,000 on your evolutionary family, there's something wrong. That's a problem. It's not, per se, true that, for example, your children deserve all your money. It's just not true. Your children deserve your support; they deserve your radical love, but because they're your biological children, it doesn't mean you should leave them all your money. You should think about *what they need, what's appropriate, and what you should leave to the rest of the world, which has a powerful and gorgeous effect.* That's how I personally spend my money, the little of it that I have. But it's a big deal.

We've got to take evolutionary family seriously. We're radically committed to them, not less than our biological families. That's a very big idea.

When we go home on Christmas, we meet our biological family. It's so important to do that, and sometimes we feel like we're kids again; sometimes, all the old stuff comes up, and all the old pain moves through us. I hope that you were able to heal some of it this Christmas, Hanukkah, and New Year and that you'll be able to heal more of it next year. Don't turn away. Never turn away from your biological family. In fact, one of my commitments this year is: *I've got to call my mom more, which I don't do often enough.*

We are radically committed to our biological families and also to our soul families. It's good to sit down and make a list: *Who's in your evolutionary family?*

- Who's in your soul print family?
- Who are your real friends?
- Who would really show up for you?
- Who would you really show up for?
- Who's in the First Principles and First Values with you together?
- Who do you have a shared vision with?

It's a big deal, so I want to just see if we can find that together. When we can find it together, we can realize who we are.

EVOLUTIONARY FAMILY FURTHERS THE GOAL OF REALITY TO GENERATE NEW FORMS OF INTIMACY

- With your evolutionary family, you don't have to play small.
- With your evolutionary family, you can be the king and queen, the prince and princess, who you really are.
- With your evolutionary family, you can confess your greatness.

Reality needs you to confess your greatness. Reality needs your service. This is such a deep idea, that Reality needs, that God needs. Reality, the Infinite, manifested the finite because the Infinite needs to give, the Infinite needs to love, and the Infinite doesn't want to have lunch alone. It's a very big deal. Infinity yearns for intimacy. Wow.

Reality needs your service, and your service comes from your greatness. When you're in your joy, you can access your greatness. That's where you find your glory.

- With your evolutionary family, confess your greatness.
- With your evolutionary family, confess your deepest heart's desire.
- With your evolutionary family, you can take your unique risk. Your unique risk might be: *I'm going to plunge into this beautiful love. I'm not sure what's going to come out of it, but I'm going to do it with such integrity that it's going to be an Outrageous Love Story.*
- With your evolutionary family, you can live your Outrageous Love Stories.

An Outrageous Love Story doesn't necessarily mean a romantic love story. It could be two sisters and two brothers. It could be beloveds who come together in a particular way or perhaps who come together forever.

- With your evolutionary family, you can take your unique

risk.

- With your evolutionary family, you can clarify and live your deepest heart's desire.
- With your evolutionary family, you can come together and form a particular quartet or symphonic movement within the great Unique Self Symphony, which is the goal of Reality: the generation of new forms of intimacy.

One of our core memes is that Reality is the progressive deepening of intimacies; that's a core structural dimension of Reality. Reality is now generating a new form of evolutionary intimacy. That's your evolutionary family. With our evolutionary families, we can live that new form of intimacy.

We can love wide, and we can love broad.

THE LAW OF HOMO AMOR IS THAT GIVING AND RECEIVING ARE ONE

Let's stand for evolutionary family and soul root family. We're not going to move through this eleventh hour of existential risk until we recognize that *my family's not just the immediate group of people around me.* No, that's not true.

My money's not mine. Anyone who thinks their money is theirs alone—that's a joke. You are invested; you're holding your finances because you're given the privilege in this world to decide where and how to distribute them according to the highest principles of wisdom.

It's not just your money but your time, resources, and energy. Your energy is not yours to hold. Your energy is a gift. I'm pouring energy into all of us, all the time.

Remember, energy is a gift, and we get to give our energy away in mad love, consistently and steadily. Give your energy a place where you're going to stay for ten, twenty, thirty, forty years—and change the world with it.

We're coming together as a revolution, as an evolutionary family, as a Planetary Awakening in Love through Unique Self Symphonies, to give the best that we are. **When we give the best we are, we receive the best the world has to offer in return.**

It's only in separate self that there's a contradiction between giving and receiving: either I'm putting money in the bank or I'm receiving money from the bank. I'm either taking money out or I'm putting money in; I'm giving, or I'm receiving. That's the law of separate self. That's the law of *Homo sapiens*.

In contrast, the law of *Homo amor*, the law of Evolutionary Unique Self, is that giving and receiving are one. That's what we mean when we say the sexual models the erotic. **In great sexuality, as in great Eros in every dimension of life, there's no split between giving and receiving.**

We're going to confess our greatness and say, *I give everything and I receive everything. That's my greatness. I'm all in.*

This is not about self-help. Self-help is about what I can get out of it. This is about the transformation of myself and Cosmos through me, which is not about what I can get out of it. It's about: *What can I pour into it?*

I'm going to give everything and I'm going to receive everything.

Happy Hanukkah, everyone. Merry Christmas. Happy New Year. Mad celebration to our evolutionary family, our soul root family.

CHAPTER NINE

INCLUDING AND TRANSCENDING: FROM BIOLOGICAL FAMILY TO SOUL ROOT EVOLUTIONARY FAMILY, PART 2

Episode 221 — January 3, 2021

JOINING TOGETHER THE DNA OF OUR UNIQUE SELVES FOR THE SAKE OF THE WHOLE

I spend Sabbath—which in the old lineage tradition of Hebrew wisdom is Friday sundown to Saturday sundown—in meditation, song, and deep study. In these weeks, I'm deep in study of the comparisons between electrical engineering and DNA. That was much of yesterday. I began looking at the structure of DNA. It's beyond shocking, the wonder of wonders of what's happening in our DNA right now, this very second—if we had even the slightest idea.

I want to invite everyone at some point this week to read about your DNA; go online and begin to study DNA. It's like, *Oh my God, wow*! **DNA is an expression of our unique singularity, our irreducible uniqueness. We call that Unique Self.**

We're going to go into uniqueness and what it means to be a Unique Self, what it means for you and me to be Unique Selves in Unique Self Symphony, and why that's the single most important dimension of information

that we could know at this moment in time because it's the answer to the question, *Who are you?*

What are we? We're a band of Outrageous Lovers. By Outrageous Lovers, we mean that we are, each of us, unique incarnations of the *LoveIntelligence*, *LoveBeauty*, and *LoveDesire* of the Cosmos—what we call Outrageous Love—that's the initiating energy and Eros of All-That-Is that lives uniquely as us.

- We come together to create a new world.
- We come together in Unique Self Symphony.
- We come together in Unique Self jazz Symphony, which means you can sense the design underneath the apparent discord. There's a "chaordic" Reality, which means chaos and order together. It's a Unique Self Symphony. Everyone's irreducibly unique, but always listening for the music of the whole.

How can I, at this moment of outrageous pain—because we live in a world of outrageous pain—realize that the only response is Outrageous Love? In the very selfsame moment, we live in a world of outrageous beauty— and that beauty's unique. Reality is waiting for each of us to be in our full, beautiful uniqueness, with so much respect for all of Reality. We are in devotion to the whole.

We are whole mates with the whole. That's another way we talk in this new set of distinctions, which is this new story. We're not just role mates with each other, but we are also soul mates and whole mates.

1. We're role mates: We have roles with each other.
2. We're soul mates: We look in each other's eyes and we're just blown away. We fall madly in love with each other. We don't limit falling in love to one person. We might fall in love in a particularly romantic way with one person—but we are also falling in love all the time. Our souls meet and it's for real.

3. We're whole mates: We're in devotion to the larger whole, together.

All of the exponential technology of DNA serves to allow us to experience the gorgeous uniqueness of each other. There's not just uniqueness in an individual; there's uniqueness in our intimate communion. **We are a community unlike any other. It doesn't make us better than any other. Uniqueness is not about,** *I'm better than you.* **It's about,** *I'm so special that I can recognize your specialness.*

But we are also special, and we're doing something that is not being done virtually anywhere else in the world.

We're coming together not as a self-help group, not to figure out, *What can I get out of this?* We're coming together for the sake of the transformation of the whole. We're coming together to make a revolution. We're literally revolutionaries. **The quality of our coming together is revolution.**

We're aware. We feel the joy and the pain of the whole. We know that we're poised between utopia and dystopia.

We experience ourselves as da Vinci and Marsilio Ficino did and that whole gang of about 1,000 people who were the heart of the Renaissance in Italy after the Black Death had swept through Europe. They also knew that they were in a time between worlds and a time between stories.

They also knew that the only response was to tell a new story—not a fanciful story, not mere conjecture, but a Story rooted in the best understandings of:

- Identity—*Who am I?*
- Community—*Who are we?*
- The Universe Story—*Where are we?*
- Action—*What is there to do? What's the next invitation? What does Cosmos want from me in the next moment?*

Da Vinci and his gang told the story of modernity, which raised all boats. But the fault lines in that story are still sinking us.

Modernity raised everything; it was a new story about the human being, divinity, and the universe—and yet *there were fault lines in the story*. These included misunderstandings of self and of Reality, which are the direct cause for the bad stories that we're living in today: the limited success stories based on win/lose metrics and rivalrous conflict, which is a key generator function for existential risk up and down the system.

- We are here in this new Renaissance.
- We are at the core of a new Renaissance, and we are da Vinci incarnate, if you will.
- We are telling a new story, but it's not about being cute (and cute is beautiful—we love cute). It's not about being sweet, or about, *Oh, I had a great experience*. Which is also beautiful, we love having great experiences, but **we are telling this story with the passion, commitment, and steadiness of revolutionaries.**

We are revolutionaries. **We want to overthrow all that doesn't work in the world order today. We do this while respecting what came before, honoring all that does work, and changing everything that needs to be changed—carefully, thoughtfully, and deeply, based on a new set of shared First Values and First Principles that are the ground of the new story, which itself is the matrix for a global ethos for a global civilization.**

Without this, an unimaginable level of suffering will continue to explode in our world, and possibly end up in extinction. With this, we can move away from dystopia towards a utopia of beauty, goodness, truth, and respect for each other—and Outrageous Love beyond imagination.

It's so good to be together, to be home here together in this revolution, with this shared commitment, with this shared passion. This is our baby. Anyone who wants to get involved, get involved. Step up, step in. Steady,

steady, steady. It's not, *What can I get today?* We're going to get everything we need from each other.

We're going to pour all of ourselves into this, and we're going to put our very breath, life, and yearning on the line and say: *We are taking our seat at the table of history.*

We are not waiting for someone else to do it. We're ready.

EVOLUTIONARY LOVE CODE: SOUL ROOT FAMILY, TRANSCENDING AND INCLUDING BIOLOGICAL FAMILY

Biological family is wondrous, and we are committed to it.

Evolutionary family, or soul root family, is not less, and sometimes even more, significant.

We need to be, at the very least, as committed to evolutionary family as we are to our biological family, and often much more so.

It is before your evolutionary family that you can confess your greatness, take your unique risk, speak and live your deepest heart's desire, and be seen in the depth of your true glory.

We will not be able to respond to existential risk without making the momentous leap from only our biological family to evolutionary and soul root family.

We have made the distinction between evolutionary family and biological family, both of which are important. This distinction itself is part of the movement of Cosmos, which moves towards the evolution of love.

The core of the Universe Story is Reality's progressive deepening of intimacies.

That's a very big sentence.

- ◆   Reality is evolution.
- ◆   Reality is relationship.
- ◆   Reality is intimacy.
- ◆   Reality is the evolution of intimacy.

It starts with subatomic particles that come together in intimate communion, and it moves all the way through the evolutionary chain up to the self-reflective human world. Then, in the human world, there are more levels of unfolding intimacy. We've talked about this before at great length, breadth, and depth.

Today, we're focusing on one dimension of the evolution of intimacy, which is the evolution from biological family to evolutionary family or soul root family.

Now, here's a key sentence: **All healthy evolution transcends and includes that which came before.** That's an important idea and a major piece in the thought of Franklin Jones, and it comes from Hegel. You negate and preserve. In other words:

There's a dimension that was limited in the old structure of consciousness. You negate it, meaning you say, that's not enough; that's a limitation, but you preserve the best in it, and then you transcend and add something undeniably new.

That's the movement of evolution. It's a very big deal.

In our code, we're talking about this emergence of a new level of intimacy: evolutionary intimacy. Let's go deeper into evolutionary or soul root family on the one hand and biological family on the other hand.

BIOLOGICAL FAMILY IS WONDROUS

Biological family is wondrous, and we're massively, completely, absolutely committed to biological family.

Evolutionary family and the soul root family are not less significant, sometimes even more so. We need to be, at the very least, as committed to our evolutionary family as we are to our biological family. It's before your evolutionary family that you confess your greatness. You take your unique risk and speak your deepest heart's desire. It's before your evolutionary family, your soul root family, that you can go the whole way in this lifetime. In your biological family, you often get caught in old patterns—you have to play small.

In your evolutionary family, you can go all the way.

We're not going to be able to respond to existential risk without making this momentous, wondrous leap in the evolution of intimacy, which is the moment that includes biological family all the way but transcends into evolutionary or soul root family.

SOUL ROOT FAMILY: WE'VE BEEN TOGETHER BEFORE

Let's talk a little more about what we mean by evolutionary and soul root family.

What do we mean by "soul root"? A soul root is a very particular idea with a very deep grounding in the great interior science traditions. Soul root means that our souls are essentially, innately connected because we come from the same root.

In one of the great images of mysticism, there are different qualities to Reality. If you remember Leonardo's figure of the human being, that famous figure, which is the human being who's mapped onto the Cosmos. That human being is actually sourced in interior science. It's called *Adam*

97

Kadmon, the primordial human. But the primordial human is really Divinity. It's the body of divinity pictured in the human body, but of course, that body of the human being includes the body of all of Reality.

- ◆ It's the body of the church.
- ◆ It's the body of Christ.
- ◆ It's the body of Buddha.
- ◆ It's the body of Mother Earth.

In the mystical traditions and interior sciences, every soul, which is my unique quality of interiority that lives beyond this world—because the evidence we have today on the continuity of consciousness is overwhelming, so to deny it, you have to be lost in materialist dogma—**comes from a different place on the divine body.** That's not a superstitious image; it's a mythic image. In this divine body, there are souls that come from the head, souls that come from the heart, souls that come from the pelvis, and souls that come from the ankles.

It's a very beautiful idea and exists in different forms in many of the great lineage traditions that *there are different soul groups.* Each of us is related to a certain soul group. *I'm related to a soul group.* When we meet someone from the same soul group, *there's a recognition between us.* There's a comfort level. **We feel at home with each other.** You meet people, that's your tribe. *These are my people. I'm home here. This is where I need to be.* Can you feel that?

That's my soul root family. It's often the case that *we've been around before.* It's a very big deal. *We've incarnated together before.*

When I mention reincarnation, I don't mention that as a woo-woo idea. I mention it having done a decade of very intensive, empirical research into the overwhelming evidence we have today on the continuity of consciousness. Read Professor Ian Stevenson from the University of Virginia, who has amassed a lot of very important data, or Professor David Ray Griffin, who's a great Whiteheadian scholar and has written on reincarnation.

So when I say "reincarnation," I mean it very intentionally. Reincarnation is very clearly a dimension of Reality. It's not over when it's over.

The people in my soul root family are people I've gone around with before. I often say to my students and beloved friends, *this lifetime I might be the teacher, and in the last lifetime you were my teacher*. In this lifetime, of course, we're all teachers and students. We're all powerful together, and we're all teaching each other. There are also certain roles that we play, but those roles might have been different in a previous lifetime. This time, I'm masculine. Last lifetime, I might have been not just feminine but female. We trade genders through lifetimes. **There's a certain essence, a certain continuity of Unique Self consciousness that's transmitted through the generations, so there's a story of my life.**

You and I, we've gone around before. The reason we feel so drawn to each other, and the reason we feel comfortable in each other's presence and at home—as well as why we're provoked by each other in sometimes very profound ways—is because we've been together before. This is not our first conversation. This is not our first rodeo. We've all been together before, and we'll all be together again. How we're together again is what we do in this lifetime.

I am a billion percent sure most of us have been together before. And we've had different relationships, which is why there are certain completions that we owe each other. **Part of a Unique Self encounter means there's unfinished business between us.**

We have to give each other dimensions of respect, integrity, love, and engagement in this lifetime in order to complete what was incomplete in a previous lifetime.

- Maybe in a previous lifetime we didn't stay, and we should have stayed.
- Maybe we needed to be loyal in a deep way, but we made pragmatic decisions. And so this lifetime, we're together to be

profoundly loyal and fix something in Cosmos.

- Maybe we betrayed each other in a previous lifetime and need to become whole in this lifetime.
- Maybe we didn't love deeply enough. We just couldn't do it. In this lifetime, we can love in a new way.
- Maybe I was childless last lifetime, and in this lifetime you're my child.

Soul root family means that we have history. We have met before. It's deeper in that sense than only the biological family of this lifetime. We may have been biological family before; we may have been soul root family before, but in any case, *We are deeply connected in our interior*. We have a debt to each other in a very deep, beautiful, and real way. We're part of an ongoing story. This is not the first chapter; we're right in the middle.

The way you can identify this is you can feel:

- I've got business with this person. I want to walk away, but I can't.
- Or I don't want to walk away. I want to stay forever. This is where I belong. This is my home. I'm willing to go all the way. Wow.

Part of our place in the world, part of our soul root family, is that we're committed to revolution. We are a group of revolutionaries. Imagine an army unit forced to make war. They come together with a level of loyalty, commitment, and grace. They've got each other's back in every way. They share in every way. All the old social status issues are erased in a foxhole.

We have some of that energy. **But we're not going to make war; we're not going to kill. We're going to give life.** We're going to become the highest peace and the highest harmony that the world can be.

We're going to create together a Unique Self Symphony. And we need each other's instruments because we're a soul root family.

ALLUREMENT OF COSMOS OVER GENERATIONS TO POSITION YOU IN YOUR BIOLOGICAL FAMILY

Biological family is not an accident or a minor detail. The allurement of Cosmos caused a series of relationships over generations, which created the conditions and the exterior and interior genetic structures that manifested you in a particular place, in a particular time, and to a particular family. That's the exact precise set of conditions that you needed to emerge and manifest your Unique Self, give your unique gift, and carry out your unique transformation. You've got an intrinsic relationship with that family, which demands loyalty and respect.

Respect is a beautiful word, and it's different from love. It's much more important to honor and respect your family than it is to love your family. Notice that in the original text of Hebrew wisdom, it doesn't say anywhere, *Love your mother and father*, or, *Love your husband or wife*. Nowhere. It says, *Honor your mother and father. Honor your partner. Respect.* **When we get to Outrageous Love, we cannot bypass respect and honor.**

I've got to respect and honor my biological family. If we get that great privilege of being deeply in love with our biological family, that's gorgeous and beautiful, and we can do an enormous piece of work there. It's an enormously important part of our lives. Sometimes that's possible, and sometimes it's not, but there's always respect and honor.

There's always completion.

There's always integrity.

There's always loyalty with my biological family, and when it really happens there can be love.

But your love is never exhausted by your biological family. When your love is exhausted by your biological family, you've turned your biological family into a modern form of idolatry: *This is the place that I love and not beyond.* That's not true. That's not what love is. Love is a quality of feeling that allows you to see clearly. **Love is a perception in which you open up and feel the other—you are intimate, and you hold them in a mutuality of pathos, a mutuality of recognition, and a mutuality of purpose.**

Sometimes, that happens with your biological family. You should have a real commitment to them. It's real and it's beautiful. Never bypass your biological family, and never bypass biology.

EVOLUTIONARY ASPECT OF SOUL ROOT FAMILY

But just as important as biology is the network, the matrix, of people that you meet along the way, who are not part of your biological root. They're part of your soul root. Evolution brought you into proximity.

The fact that we have widespread social mobility today and the fact that we can travel—between countries, socioeconomic classes, religions, and nationalities—and we can find each other soul to soul, heart to heart, interior to interior—*that matters greatly*. That's what it means to be worldcentric. I'm part of the community of men and women in the world, and there are Unique Self encounters along the way that I feel particularly drawn to, that I'm particularly allured to.

I'm allured. I'm drawn. There's something to be done here. Sometimes we get married, and sometimes we split up afterward.

If I'm in the biological family world: We came together. We created a family, man and wife—which is an expression of the biological world because we have children—and then when we get divorced, we split up. Then we change the locks, we throw each other out, and we demonize each other. No, no, no. *If we were drawn together sufficiently to have a relationship, oh my God, that means we're part of the same evolutionary family.* Maybe for a period of time, we're meant to be married, and maybe for the time afterward we're not, but *we're together.*

We're part of the same soul root story.

If I'm allured to you, if we came together, if we met, we've got to be loyal to that meeting. But then there are those people we didn't just meet once but who *we're deeply connected to. We find each other in a deep way. That's my* real evolutionary family. *We're whole mates. We're not just role mates and not just soul mates, but* **we're whole in and of ourselves—together for the sake of the whole.**

That quality of being whole mates together for the sake of the whole, that quality of communion that comes from participating together in the evolutionary impulse, is unlike anything else. That quality of Eros and intimacy that comes from sharing a vision, looking at the same horizon, being committed to the same revolution, feeling the same suffering and outrageous pain, being committed to the same Outrageous Love, holding hands together, knowing that we need each other's instrument in the Unique Self Symphony, hearing each other's instruments—that creates a loyalty between us and an integrity that's unimaginable.

That's the band of Outrageous Lovers.

We have to give *our all* to each other.

- Sometimes, *our all* means my full feeling and presence.
- Sometimes, *our all* means *I show up with an enormous amount of time.* I don't just ration my time: *How much time am I giving this? Am I getting paid or not getting paid?* I show up, and I give the resource of my time, which is invaluable, and I pour in my energy and time because this is my family.
- Sometimes, *our all* means I pour in my finances because *this is my family.*

Whenever someone's doing their last will and testament, I suggest that if they have enough funds to help their children so they can get set up, so they can get started in the world, that's beautiful—many of us don't have that; I didn't receive any funds like that—but if you have that, that's a blessing. *But don't leave everything to your children. That's a disaster.* They don't need it. Rather, *redistribute it*. Figure out where you can best impact, figure out where your soul root family is, where your evolutionary family is.

The word for money is *kesef* in the original Hebrew, which relates to *kissufin*, yearning. It's what we truly yearn for. Often, I've given enormous amounts of money—within the limited amount of money that I have, to be clear, but— disproportionate amounts of income to people who are part of my soul root family because that was the right thing to do at that moment in time.

We stand for each other.

We're at home. We're each other's home. We become each other's home in some profound way.

This is a very big deal.

- ◆ We're a planetary community of evolutionary souls.
- ◆ We're a band of Outrageous Lovers. But at the core, we're a family.
- ◆ We're a family that's committed to a revolution.
- ◆ We stand for each other as familiar in that deep sense of profound intimacy.
- ◆ We're willing to put everything on the line for each other.

That's what it means to show up. That's what it means to create evolutionary intimacy. The way we're going to create the Unique Self Symphony, which is the next stage of the self-organizing universe, is to have that experience: *I'm going to show up for you all the way. I'm going to lay it all on the line for you, not just for my son, my uncle, my daughter, or for the person who's my partner.*

Yes, for all of those—those are gorgeous. But it doesn't end there. My soul root family, my evolutionary family, is just as important. And I want to show up all the way.

I AM NOT WILLING TO BE WRITTEN IN THE BOOK OF LIFE WITHOUT YOU

I want to end with a story, with your permission. It's a story that we've been telling here together for the last ten or twelve years. Maybe the story will make sense in a whole different way.

It's a story about a master on the holiest day of the year in which there was a decision to be made, and the decision was who shall live and who shall die. Some of you may remember that song by Leonard Cohen, "Who Shall Live and Who Shall Die?" That was the decision to be made in that lineage on that day.

It's an incredible decision. A year ago, in January 2020, we asked, *Who shall live and who shall die*? No one imagined that 1.8 million people around the world would die, 300,000 people in America, tens of thousands of people in France and people in Cuba, Asia, England, Belgium, Holland, China, and all over the world. We could not imagine that we were going to lose an entire group of people, that so many of them would die alone, and that there would be so many side effects that would cause cascading waves of depression, death, pain, and breakdown. That there'd be so many people out of breath, literally.

Who shall live and who shall die? We have no idea what this next year will bring.

We're committed to bringing life and revolution, and we're committed to joy all the way. So listen to this story of this master.

He says, *When we're here together, and we say at the beginning of this New Year, who shall live and who shall die? There's a way to transcend, and, if you will, to defeat the angel of death.*

Everyone says, *How? How?* The master says, *We can do it if we're willing to look at each other—and not just at our biological families—and say to each other, "I'm not willing to be written in the Book of Life without you."* Wow.

That's my unique risk: I am not willing to be written in the Book of Life without you. When I say that, the angel of death is confused because the ego self has disappeared. The angel of death can only take the soul of a person living in their ego self.

Evolutionary family has been born. Soul print family has been born. This new emergence of evolutionary intimacy has been born in the world. And *bila ha'ma'vet la'netzach*: "Death at some level is transcended."

If you're up for it, as we step in to evolve the source code, as we stand poised between utopia and dystopia and attempt to tell the new story, we can say, *I am not willing to be written in the Book of Life without you.*

When that happens, in the words of the mystics, *bila ha'ma'vet la'netzach*, we transcend death.

It's a big risk, but it's beautiful—and *it's the essence of who we are.*

That's what it means to be a band of Outrageous Lovers.

CHAPTER TEN

THE BLESSING OF THE FATHER: THE PERSONAL, THE POLITICAL, THE COSMIC

Episode 338 — April 22, 2023

THE CHAPTER OF THE FATHER

It's a very moving day.

It's a very moving day because a lot is moving in the world, a lot is moving in me personally, a lot is moving in you, in *we*, in us. A lot is moving.

Who are we? How do we locate ourselves in what's moving?

I am particularly moving *physically*. I am in Texas. I got here a few days ago, from a very, very deep dive. I had done a couple of days in Sedona, where I did a deep dive with a group of about twenty *beyond awesome* human beings, where I was sharing, friending, and doing some tender teaching. It was a very sacred time, and I expected to go to Austin to record a bunch of programs with a beautiful man, who is a dear friend and partner. He studies with me as a Hebrew wisdom initiate, which is a great joy for both of us, and at the same time he's activating a beautiful world emergent from his own journeys over the last twenty years, in a stunning way—Aubrey Marcus.

As we landed together in Austin, a couple of hours later, he got a phone call that his dad had died. It was completely sudden and unexpected. Normally, with someone who is as

completely close to me as Aubrey, I would have gotten on the phone and would have done a deep-dive Holy of Holies and of course, flown to the funeral—but here I was, actually in his house.

As the Intimate Universe wove it, there we were together, in the death of the father.

I did not know how to engage it or how to approach it—the particulars of Aubrey's father, what that story is, and that particular personal story of the death of the father. I wasn't sure how to approach it, how to create the space for Aubrey personally, what he needed, the depth of his heart's desire and the desire of Cosmos—in part because his father story is a tragic story—and a celebratory story, and a beautiful story. It's a *holy and broken Hallelujah* story.

Clearly, we immediately canceled all the programs we had planned. We embraced for a moment in tears late in the night and went to sleep. I woke up, still not knowing anything. I stepped into the shower, and in the shower, sometimes holy things happen. I closed my eyes and **I just felt this whisper and saw this vision of what could emerge—the words** *blessings of the father* **whispered in my ear, and** *She* **began to weave a new piece of an already emergent vision, critical for what we're doing here at One Mountain**. I went downstairs and shared the vision with Aubrey. He sensed it immediately, and we were both all in—and the rest of the time I was there were days of intensity, magic, and miracles.

To get a sense of something of what happened, I tenderly invite anyone who would like, to listen to our podcast where we tried to describe it.

That's what I'd like to talk to you about a little bit today.

Generally speaking, what is One Mountain, Many Paths? And what are we doing here? We are saying that in order to respond to the meta-crisis effectively, we have to tell a New Story of Value rooted in First Principles and First Values, activated through first practices. In other words:

- The *dharma*—the First Principles and First Values, the Story of Value—needs yoga.
- First practices need First Principles.

That's unbelievably important. Fichte and Schelling were unbelievably important figures in Germany around the time of Hegel and Schopenhauer. They were very brilliant teachers, and there was a fifty-year heyday in Germany of emergent spirituality, a kind of proto-evolutionary spirituality. However, all of it disappeared because the dharma wasn't full enough; there wasn't a deeper Story of Value. There were First Principles and First Values, but there weren't first practices.

So when we come together here in One Mountain:

- We pray together, and we reclaim prayer at a higher level of consciousness.
- We come, and we retell the story of human history.
- We articulate, capture, vision, and recover not only a memory of the past, the best and most validated leading-edge insights of the entire traditional, modern, and postmodern world— but also a memory of the future.
- We integrate those insights, and we actually tell a new Story of Value.

It's only a new story that changes history.

I am going to try to add a dimension to the story this week, to add a new chapter to the story.

I am at Aubrey's ranch outside of Austin, and people are gathering from all over the world. Literally, right after this One Mountain, I'm going to officiate at the funeral, and we are going to do a several-hour funeral service for Aubrey's dad.

But we are going to not just honor Aubrey's dad and engage in the death of his father, but also talk about **the death of the Father in culture**.

And what does it mean to reclaim the Father?

And what does it mean to restore the Father?

And what does it mean to evolve the Father?

And what does it mean to receive the Blessing of the Father?

THE DECONSTRUCTION OF VALUE IS ALSO THE DECONSTRUCTION OF THE FATHER

We all have a father. Everyone here has a father. Even if we were conceived through artificial insemination, there was still an original father. So there's the relationship to the father—**but the relationship to the father has gotten lost.**

- ◆ The father doesn't quite know what it means to be a father.
- ◆ The son and daughter and the father don't quite know how to relate to each other, and there is this enormous alienation between the father and the child.
- ◆ The father doesn't quite know his role.

We have talked a lot in the last couple of years about the mother—the mother is unbelievably important. But today, the focus is the father.

The father doesn't know his role, he doesn't know what he is supposed to be doing.

In the old world, the primary responsibility of the father was to be the protector and the transmitter of value. But today, in the postmodern world, value has been deconstructed—and if value has been deconstructed, well, then what's the role of the father? **We have interrupted the transmission of value**.

The father is the biological father, and the father is the teacher, and the father is the system of governance, and the father is Spirit, and the father is religion at its best. Governance, religion, spirit, and literature, at its best, can also be part of the voice of the Father.

> *The voice of the Father is the mechanism that transmits value from one generation to the next.*

The father lives in the personal: the personal father. Then, there is the Father in culture, and **the Father in culture is *value*.** The Father in culture is living inside of a home, which has structure and First Principles and First Values.

We've lost that. The death of the Father is both personal and cultural.

The personal and the cultural are deeply related. Early feminism wasn't wrong when it said the personal is the political. Let's say it just a little bit differently: **The personal is the cultural.**

The role of the father has collapsed. The father's role used to be to transmit value to the next generation and transmit a commitment to fulfill your role:

- To be a good woman, whatever that meant 100 or 200 years ago (which seemed to be relatively clear).
- To be a good man, whatever that once meant.

There was relative clarity, even if that clarity was often degraded. The role of the feminine was in many ways degraded, as was the role of the masculine. We didn't have a sense of the depth of the masculine and the depth of the feminine.

So **the father transmitted the values of culture, and he also transmitted, *underneath* the values of culture, that there actually *was* real value—and he stood for that value.** But when value has been deconstructed, what's the role of the father?

The deconstruction of value is also the deconstruction of the Father.

We need to restore the Father.

But we're not going back to the old Father, to the *regressive* Father. We need the *evolutionary* Father, the *new* Father.

That's what we want to talk about today: the Blessing of the Father. We want to first do two things:

1. We want to show that **this is absolutely central in culture**, though often hidden in today's cultural codes.
2. We want to show that there is a new moment that's emerging. **There is a new relationship between child and father that hasn't existed before**—it's been nascent, and it's been growing. We want to look at that relationship, both personally—in each of us—and culturally—in all of us.

We want to tell the new story of the Father, in order to receive the Blessing of the Father.

EVOLUTIONARY LOVE CODE: BLESSING OF THE FATHER

We need the Blessings of the Father.

We need to reclaim the Father, to restore the Father, to fix the Father, to evolve the Father. Not only the Father below, but also the Father above, and within all.

We need the Blessings of the Mother. We need to reclaim the Mother, restore the Mother, fix the Mother, and evolve the Mother. Not only the Mother below, but also the Mother above, and within all.

The Mother needs the Father, and the Father needs the Mother. We need the Mother and the Father. We participate in the Mother and the Father. For 2,000 years, we have dethroned the Mother. Only in the last 100 years has the Mother begun to be reclaimed.

Today, the Western world is murdering the Father. This is the age of the death of the Father in the West, and we need to resurrect and evolve the Father.

STAR WARS: A SON WHO DOESN'T KNOW WHO HIS FATHER IS

How do you see that this issue of the Father is at the center of culture? Let's see if we can look at this in a bunch of ways.

One of the ways that culture speaks is through its *texts around the campfire*—and the texts around the campfire these days are, more often than not, *movies*. These cinematic texts of culture often speak louder than the intended articulation of the producers, the directors, or the writers. **In some sense, the whisper of *She*, the whisper of evolutionary emergence, the whisper of Eros that wants to shape, reshape, and reweave culture, speaks through the texts of cinema.**

What is the most oft-viewed contemporary story in culture in the last fifty years?

The answer unquestionably is *Star Wars,* by George Lucas. This huge story, with far-flung reaches, with spin-off after spin-off, with three trilogies and a few independent movies, sets of *Star Wars* books and TV series, and other movies focused on Boba Fett, Obi-Wan, and others—this story is the very center of culture.

Now, friends, what is the center of the story? The center of the story, as Episode Four of *Star Wars* begins, is **a son who doesn't know who his father is.**

His name is Luke Skywalker, and he has this realization that the father he is living with is not his real father. The father he is living with is a beautiful man, but Luke has this yearning to find *Source*. He has this yearning to find the father—because in this case, his biological father is not only biological, but in some sense, he's actually his source. That's not always true, but in this story, it clearly is. So he needs to find his father, but his father can't be found. In fact, his father, who used to be called Anakin Skywalker, is actually the right hand of Emperor Palpatine, and his name is Darth Vader.

Luke is searching for the father, and he desperately wants the father. He wants to meet and recognize the father. In order to get the Blessing of the Father, the relationship between father and son has to change. He cannot rely on the father to be the protector.

He has to find the father.

He has to liberate the father.

> *Not only does the son need the father,*
> *but the father needs the son.*

That's the central story of *Star Wars*. The first trilogy is essentially about Luke Skywalker realizing that Darth Vader is the father and his refusal to kill the father. Obi-Wan and Yoda say, *You have to kill Darth Vader*. Luke says, *No, I won't kill him.* **He refuses to kill the father, and instead, he comes to liberate the father.**

Do you understand what just happened, friends?

In order for him to get the Blessing of the Father, he needs to liberate the father, to have his father look at him face-to-face—and in that moment of face-to-face, there's the Blessing of the Father, which is the last scene of Episode Six in the first trilogy, when Darth Vader takes his mask off, and we realize this is Anakin Skywalker. We knew it intellectually, but Anakin Skywalker, the spark of Anakin, returns in his final moments, in his last breaths.

All of this is provoked, all of this is accomplished by who? By Luke Skywalker, the son. The son liberates the father.

We don't yet know the other dimensions of the story. We don't yet know who Anakin's father is.

In fact, one of the deep and complex questions of *Star Wars* is: Where did Anakin come from? If you remember, we know his mother, but we don't know who the father is. It's a kind of immaculate conception; he's *The One*. Anakin Skywalker is the one who can shift the balance of Cosmos. He's the one who can bring wholeness to The Force. But who the father is, we don't know. I'm not going to enter this territory now, but there are about five or six subtle hints interlaced throughout Episodes One through Six that suggest that either Palpatine or more likely, Palpatine's teacher, Darth Plagueis, may well have been Anakin's father.

The absence of the father is devastating for Anakin, so he can't quite locate himself in the Field of Value—he's torn between competing fathers. For example, Episode Three of the second trilogy begins with Anakin, together with Obi-Wan, rescuing Palpatine (who they don't yet know is a Sith Lord).

- There's a whole set of scenes in which Obi-Wan is seemingly the father to Anakin: he's his teacher, he's the father figure.
- There's another set of scenes (all in the first sixty minutes of Episode Three) in which Yoda seems to be the father figure.
- But then, there's a third set of scenes, in which the most powerful figure emerges, Palpatine, who becomes the dominant father figure. Because Anakin cannot locate himself in the Field of Value, he's not sure who the father is—and Palpatine seduces him to the dark side.

We're not going to do a deep analysis of *Star Wars* and read it as a sacred cultural text, in the way that we sometimes do. I just want to touch on it for a second, to realize that **the central myth of the last fifty years in culture, the story told most often, is about the Father**.

It's about the yearning for the Father.

It's about the yearning for the Blessing of the Father, and it's about the son needing to go find the Father.

The son liberates the Father, and then the Father can give his Blessing.

When I say *the son*, I mean the son and the daughter. It's actually Luke and Leia, who's the daughter. There's a son and a daughter.

Just feel that in terms of the personal, feel that in terms of the cultural, and feel that in terms of the cosmic.

THIS IS WHERE I LEAVE YOU: THE FATHER IS NO LONGER SPEAKING

There is a new (or relatively new) Jane Fonda movie on Netflix, *This Is Where I Leave You.*

It's about a father who's died. He has a number of children. Fonda is the wife and the mother, and she tells the children that their father has demanded that they all come together after his death and sit *shiva*, which means "seven," as in "seven days." *Shiva* also means "the oath"—the oath that the child swears to the father. Sitting *shiva* is a psychotechnology of the Hebrew lineage, where we sit in the mourner's house and tell stories of the father or the mother (we only sit *shiva* when a mother or a father has died). So, Jane Fonda tells the children—who are all grown adults, all in very complex lives with very complex relationships with their partners or non-partners, with complex relationships between the kids—she tells them, *Your father said you all have to sit shiva.*

But then you realize that the father never said this. The mother is pretending he did, which is very significant because the subtle point in the movie is that **the father has lost his voice**. In other words:

- The father is no longer commanding.
- The father is no longer gathering the children.
- The father dies silent, without saying anything.
- The father no longer has a voice, so Jane Fonda, who's the mother, has now stepped in.

Now again, all power to the Blessing of the Mother and the emergence of the feminine, the ascension of the feminine, in all of the most beautiful ways. We've talked about that for many years, and I've written a number of books on the feminine, but that's not our conversation now.

The Mother has emerged over the last 100 years—and we have murdered the Father.

There's been a murder of the Father, and in fact, the murder of the Father causes murder.

My dear friend Warren Farrell, who's the Vice President at our Center and holding the entire field of family and gender, wrote a book called *The Boy Crisis*. One of the things he's pointed out is **every school shooter in America shares one thing in common: they have no relationship to the father**. It's totally shocking. I don't want to debate now whether it's the cause or just correlation, but I think that it's unbelievably important. We know that the lack of a stable relationship with the father causes a breakdown in the son or the daughter, in a way that is unimaginably significant.

In the last sixty to seventy years, we have learned about attachment. Attachment theory is about attachment to early caretakers, but the focus is usually on the mother, and how the nature of the relationship to the mother affects how the child emerges in the early weeks and months of their life. But it's not only the relationship to the mother; it's also the relationship to the father. **When there is no father, then something collapses in the daughter and the son.**

But the father and mother are not only the father and mother of the nuclear family. When we allow the nuclear family to become our entire Field of Value, and we abandon our larger vision, our larger sense of the whole, and our larger relationship to the whole, then the nuclear family itself becomes a form of idolatry.

Beware of the explosion of the nuclear family! When the nuclear family *replaces* our larger vision and our larger dream, instead of being an *expression of* that dream, then ultimately, we explode, and something explodes in the family.

- We're not just talking about the mother and the father *in the nuclear family*.
- We're talking about the Mother and more specifically, this week, the Father more broadly *in culture*.

In *This Is Where I Leave You*, this very subtle move—that the father never really said, "gather the children for shiva"—was made by the writers, likely without intention. This was just a little clever dramatic ploy: *Oh, she made it up*. But actually, it's very significant, and this is how culture speaks. It's saying: **The father is no longer speaking. The father no longer transmits (value) to the children**.

WHALE: THE DAUGHTER LIBERATES THE FATHER

One movie that won an Oscar this year is *Whale*, which is a story of a father and his daughter. She feels that she's been abandoned by the father. The father is reaching for the daughter, but he cannot quite find her. He can't quite find her joy, and she can't find his joy. The movie chronicles the last four or five days of the father's life.

He is a whale, meaning he's extremely large. He's large because his beloved died, and he has lost connection to his daughter. Eros has gone out of his life, but the emptiness is so painful that he covers it up with pseudo-eros, which for him is food. In the last twenty minutes of the movie, there's an incredible scene of him eating, this pseudo-erotic stuffing and tragic, pseudo-erotic bloating.

He bloats and bloats and bloats, as he gets smaller and smaller and more contracted inside.

The daughter says to him somewhere in the middle of the movie, *take three steps towards me*. He can barely get up, and he can't do it. The final scene in the movie is when they actually do find each other, and they recover their joy, and they recover the father and the daughter. And he takes three steps towards her, and then there's this light.

She remembers, he remembers.

The movie ends, and we feel that this was his last moment, the death of the father.

The movie ends with the death of the father—but importantly, it ends with **the death of the father *after* the father has been liberated**. He desperately wants to give the Blessing of the Father to his daughter, but she needs to challenge him, and she needs to liberate him. The daughter needs the father, but the father also needs the daughter—so it's a new relationship.

It's a new relationship, a new partnership, where the daughter liberates the father in order for the him to give the blessing to the daughter—and he cannot die without having given the Blessing of the Father.

So that's already the third movie. This is literally written in the story of culture itself.

EVERYTHING EVERYWHERE ALL AT ONCE: THE ULTIMATE POSTMODERN TRAGEDY

What other movie won an Oscar this year? It actually picked up seven Oscars. *Everything Everywhere All at Once*. What's that movie about? That movie is about the death of the Father in culture.

I saw the movie in the theater, and I got up in the middle of the movie and walked out because I was literally sick to my stomach. And then I went and watched the rest of the movie later, in order to be able to talk about it with you.

I am not going to talk about it in depth now, but I'll just say for now, **that movie is the ultimate postmodern tragedy**. The essential point of the movie is that there is no intrinsic value anywhere. That's what the movie is about.

- It moves through the multiverse.
- Nothing makes sense. Everything is disjointed.
- There is no narrative arc.
- There is no intrinsic value.
- There is no grand narrative of culture or value.
- Everything is everywhere, all at once.
- No vector. No Eros that's real.
- No telos, no direction, no plotline.

And then there's this arbitrary decision at the end of the movie: *Okay, well, we might as well just be good, just because, although there's no ground of value.* This is the classic existentialist move. That's Sartre. That's Camus. Existentialism is, as it were, proto-postmodernist.

The movie begins with them leaving the father. The father is Gong Gong, who lives in the Orient. They need to leave him because Gong Gong is the oppressive father, and the oppressive father is the symbol, in the movie, for the degraded Father.

- We no longer have a father who is a source of value.
- We no longer have a father who gives blessings.

They flee the father.

Fleeing from the father to the West and into its postmodern deconstruction of value, is what the movie is about. And value in culture *is* the Father, so the point of the movie is there is no value.

We've run away from the Father; the Father was degraded.

We now live in a multiverse, without direction, without plotline, without narrative arc, without meaning.

The Father has died. And you can feel the *un-We*, which is George Steiner's word for the current pervasive sense of meaninglessness.

AVATAR: KILLING OF THE DEGRADED FATHER

The next movie is *Avatar*, which we've talked about extensively on One Mountain.[1]

Avatar I, again, begins with the death of the father. And who is the father? There are actually two fathers.

One is culture. **Governance is the father.** Jake Sully is wounded in a war for value that's not value, for expansionist colonial humanity—and yet, the government won't give him money to fix his legs. His legs *can* be fixed so he can walk, but the father doesn't protect him. The father sends him to a meaningless war and then doesn't take care of him. There are clips that were edited out of the movie, but they are available online, of Jake Sully, the key protagonist in the movie, talking about how the government didn't take care of him. So there is no father in this sense.

When his brother dies, he joins this Avatar project in which human beings inhabit bodies from the planet Pandora, which has a particular mineral called *unobtainium*, which is enormously valuable and can tilt the balance of power on Earth.

The second father in the film is Jake's **new father figure**, Miles Quaritch, the Marine colonel. He's a father figure, and he says to Jake, *I'll get your legs fixed, I'll take care of you.* The father. But he's a regressive father, an ethnocentric father. His ethnocentrism is not based on a nation-state like China, the United States, Russia, or the Philippines. His ethnocentrism is human-based. He believes humans are truly valuable; all the other galactic species are, in some sense, subhuman and should be treated as such. That's another version of the degraded father.

So the government fails as father, and then you've got the degraded father in Miles Quaritch. So what Jake needs to do is **kill the father**. In this movie,

---

1 See, for example, "Is Value Real?" One Mountain, Many Paths, Episode 325, https://medium.com/office-for-the-future/325-is-value-real-the-oracle-of-open-ai-avatar-and-the-field-of-value-a-memory-of-two-futures-9c7393fa1885.

the father has to be killed, and in the end, it's Jake, and particularly Neytiri, the Na'vi princess he meets in his Avatar body, who kills Miles Quaritch.

It's the killing of the Father—but it's the killing of the regressive father, the killing of the degraded father.

There's one other father figure in *Avatar I*: Neytiri's father, Eytukan. He's the one true father in the film. When Neytiri wants to go ethnocentric and reject Jake, the father is wise and says: *No, we take Jake, and he learns the ways of our people.* In other words, there has to be an opening here; there has to be a possibility here—we have to open up new possibilities. He's a visionary, Eytukan.

That's *Avatar I*.

AVATAR: THE WAY OF WATER: THE SON SAVES THE FATHER

I'm going to do one last one, and it's beautiful and stunning: *Avatar II*. This movie has a number of through-lines, but the most important ones are about the father and the son.

Number one, Miles Quaritch, who had been killed by Neytiri in *Avatar I*, survives because his memories were uploaded into a new Na'vi body as part of his Avatar project. In that sense, he has, as it were, been resurrected. So Miles Quaritch is back on the scene. His son, Spider, the son of the biological Miles Quaritch, had been left behind on Pandora. One vector of the movie is their relationship. Spider hates the father, but there's the slow emergence of a relationship between them, and particularly, **the son liberates the father**. The father captures Spider, thinking he'll use him in order to find and kill Jake Sully—but in his memory, in the deep-essence psyche of Miles Quaritch, there is this father's love of the son.

As with Darth Vader, there is this sense of the father who still loves the son—so when the Emperor, Palpatine, goes to kill Luke with his blue lightning, and Luke screams, *Father, Father!*, it's that screaming that finally liberates Anakin Skywalker from the metallic technological encasing of Darth Vader. And then he saves Luke by killing Palpatine (or so we think) to restore balance to The Force.

The same thing happens in *Avatar II*. The father's love for Spider still stirs in Miles Quaritch, and Spider begins to teach his father. His father watches Spider, and Spider evokes something new in him: he evokes compassion, love, and a new ethic.

Towards the end of the movie, Miles Quaritch is unconscious underwater, and who saves the father? **The son saves the father.** Spider saves his father.

But they don't merge together. Miles Quaritch says, *now come with me.* And Spider says *no, we don't share a Field of Value.* But there's the beginning of a relationship, and the future Avatar movies undoubtedly will play with that.

The second theme in *Avatar II* is the relationship between the father and mother, Neytiri and Jake Sully, and their children, particularly the relationship between Lo'ak, the second son, and Jake.

Jake doesn't *see* his son, who is enormously gifted and desperate for the Blessing of the Father. But he doesn't know how to find the Blessing of the Father, and Jake doesn't know how to find the blessing. He doesn't even realize he's not giving it.

- ◆ It's Lo'ak who has the wider vision.
- ◆ It's Lo'ak who sees something no one else sees.
- ◆ It's Lo'ak who creates a relationship with the giant sea whales, without whom, ultimately, the day couldn't be saved.
- ◆ It's Lo'ak who saves Jake Sully and liberates him from his near-certain death underwater.

There's this key scene at the end, in which Lo'ak and Jake see each other, and they say, *I see you.* Just like the scene in which Spider says to the resurrected Miles Quaritch, *I see you.*

So do you begin to see this, friends?

I just invoked six themes, six engagements with the father, just to show you: **it's always right in front of us and we can't see it. It's at the very center of culture today.**

At the very center of culture, we have this conversation about the Father.

THE SON NEEDS THE FATHER, AND THE FATHER NEEDS THE SON

Let us go one more huge step and locate it even more deeply. The primary religious story in Western civilization is the Christ story. What's the Christ story about? **It's about the Father who needs the Son.** Does everyone get that? It's wild!

The Father is all-powerful. The Father is the Infinity of Power, and yet the Father needs the Christ. The Father needs the Son.

The Son feels abandoned by the Father. When Jesus is on the cross, he's famously reported to have said: *Forgive them, Father, for they know not what they do.* But in a second version of the New Testament, there's this other dimension, as Jesus says: *Eloi, Eloi, lema azavtani: My God, My God, my Father, my Father, why have you forsaken me?*

Are you beginning to see this?

We are looking for the Blessing of the Father.

There is a way in which we've murdered the father: **We have murdered *value*, and the father instantiates, represents, and incarnates value.**

- ◆ We need the father.
- ◆ We need the Blessing of the Father.
- ◆ But the father also needs the son.

It's this new moment, where the son needs the father, and the father needs the son. And by *the son*, I mean the son and the daughter. The son and the daughter need the father; the father needs the son and the daughter.

There's this new emergent partnership between:

- The Divine Father, the evolving Field of Value,
- And humanity participating in the evolution of that Field of Value.

Value that lives within us evolves and completes the Father.

We liberate the Father.

We *participate* in the evolution of value, which is the evolution of God—and the Father *holds* the Field of Value. **The Father holds, animates, calls, and personally addresses us, inviting us, and demanding that we fulfill our unique destinies as sons and daughters.**

It's a new moment in history, and in this new moment in history, there's this new emergence.

That's what we mean by conscious evolution.

What we mean by conscious evolution is that we're awakening to the realization that the evolutionary process lives in us. When we become conscious as human beings and realize that we have the power of ancient gods, that we can directly affect evolutionary history.

- We can affect the evolution of love.
- We can affect the evolution of value.
- We can affect the evolution of consciousness.

We can affect it in the most beautiful and transformative ways. However:

- If we lose access to our Field of Value
- If we lose access to the Good, the True, and the Beautiful, as they live in us, because we've murdered the Father, we've

murdered the Father in ourselves

Then we *degrade* the Field of Value. There is this unimaginable, inexplicable, mysterious new moment in history, in which the father needs the son, and the son needs the father. The father needs the daughter, and the daughter needs the father.

This is the moment of the Anthropocene, in which the human being takes a central role, but that central role makes no sense without holding hands with the Father and being embraced by the Mother.

Today, we are focusing on the Father.

- The Father means: I am in the Field of Value.
- The Father means: I am called.
- The Father means: There is a sense of unique obligation.

Now, here's the thing: the personal father and the cosmic Father, the personal father and the Father which is the Field of Value—they are deeply related.

In other words, the way I conceive the Field of Value, the Divine Field of Value, often has an enormous amount to do with the way I conceive my father and my relationship to the Father, and my relationship to the Mother. **So we have to do our personal work—both to liberate ourselves from the father and receive the Blessing of the Father at the same time.**

That's the paradox. Abraham has to liberate himself from the father in order to articulate a new vision, and yet he also needs the Blessing of the Father. He doesn't get it from his biological father, so he returns to the Father in culture. He turns to the Father, our Father in heaven.

But in the end, we need both.

We need to do our best to understand our relationship to our personal father, to heal what can be healed. Sometimes, it can be healed, and sometimes it can't—that's also sometimes true. But we are in this new moment in relationship to the Father. We need to reclaim the Father, the dignity of the Father, the value that the Father instantiates. The father needs the son, and the son needs the father.

This begins a new chapter in the emergence of the new human and new humanity—the restoration and evolution of the Father.

I hope this was helpful and valuable to you. The reason I went through this wide view of culture, through these six cinematic texts, is to get the sense that I'm not making this up. It's right in front of us, and we often can't see it.

The Father is absolutely central to everything. This new moment of the Father is just emerging, and we need to tell a new story of the Father.

We're weaving culture together.

CHAPTER ELEVEN

THE INTIMACY CRISIS: WHY THE ATLANTIC MAGAZINE GOT IT WRONG

Episode 342 — May 7, 2023

RECEIVE THE INVITATION OF THIS MOMENT

Someone left me a message this morning, suggesting this image, and it was so true and correct:

It is twenty years from now—or thirty or forty or fifty or sixty—and everything we've been talking about here for the last ten years—this meta-crisis, which we've entered into deeply and diagnosed as a global intimacy disorder—imagine that all of the possibilities that we said *might* happen, *have happened*, and we are actually on the verge of the last collapse, and we are right before a moment where we cross the Rubicon into some dystopian scenario, either into some version of extinction, the death of humanity or the death of our humanity.

Then we're offered this time machine, which allows us to go back and be right here in 2023—to act and make a new set of decisions. What decisions would we make?

Today, we're going to enter deeply into this next step in the revolution, this next step in understanding what it means:

- To respond to the meta-crisis.
- To be alive and in full incarnation of Eros and delight.

128

- To celebrate.

We are going to enter into the world of story:

- The world of live your story
- The world of story as a structure of Cosmos
- The world of reshape and re-vision your story
- The world of choose your story
- The world of own your story
- The world of "edit" your story
- The world of *God loves stories*

It's an enormously important day, and this is a wildly critical and gorgeous new expression. We are going to be weaving together pieces from the past twenty years, but with a new sense and feeling. And by the end of today, my promise—*Her* promise, our promise, our promise to each other—is that if we stay in full focus, we will return to ourselves today—each of us—a piece of our story that's gotten lost.

But the first step—and I want to introduce it as our intention-setting to-day—is radical *kavanah*.

Radical kavanah means full, potent, unimaginable focus. Focus means that we are sensitive and responsive to the invitation and the need of this moment.

One of the saddest things for me is when I would sometimes talk to a person who I feel is deep *in*, we are standing beside each other for a year, for two years, for five years—and then they'll say something, and I realize: *Wow, they just don't get it.* They are looking at this meta-crisis, our response, and this telling of a new Story of Value in response to the meta-crisis as a kind of hobby. It's a hobby we do; it gives us a sense of meaning, entertains us somewhat, and gives us a sense of belonging—but basically, this is *not* where our focus is. Our focus is on a thousand other things, diffused to a thousand other engagements—and some of them are important and holy and should be attended to—but ultimately, this is just this little slice of what we do, a nice ornament. It's a nice piece of jewelry in our lives.

That's exactly *not* where we need to be.

That's what this exercise is:

- Imagine we could come back to this time.
- And we could choose differently.
- And we know that our choices can actually shift the very vector of history itself.

There is no question in my mind that they can't. If you doubt that a small group of people can come together and change history, which is *his*-story/ *her*-story—it's not true. We can.

The *only* thing that ever changes history is when a small group of people come together and become a spiritual society, a band of Outrageous Lovers. They become an intimate communion with evolutionary longing and yearning, holding each other in mad love, through the potency and poignancy, and through the promise and pain—and together, we tell a New Story of Value that potentiates, that is potent, throbbing, tumescent, dripping, and alive: a story that births the New World.

It's only the radical focus, the radical placing of attention, that allows us to tell the New Story of Value, to receive the whispers of She, to spread ourselves open.

To spread our hearts, and our embodiment, and our souls open, to receive the penetration of this moment, to receive the invitation of this moment, to so focus on the moment that we can enter it fully, we can penetrate it fully, and throb it alive.

IT TAKES A THOUSAND *NO*'S TO SAY *YES*

We live in this moment of attention hijacking, where our attention is hijacked in a thousand directions. We can't quite focus. There are too many options, too many possibilities, and too much scrolling happening—and we need to get quiet, go inside, and feel: **who am I?**

Am I a private soul?

A private soul means my job is to take care of me and my family—which is beautiful; everyone needs to take care of me and my family—but if I'm really awake to who I am, I realize I am not just a private soul.

I am a public soul.

A public soul doesn't always mean acting in public. My friend wrote to me this weekend about a set of choices she's made, which are all private choices, but they were the choices of a public soul. The choices were to study deeply, and not to worry about degrees, diplomas, or public structures of success. All these trappings are often not expressions of a public soul but of a private soul governed by win/lose metrics.

To really be a public soul means to study, learn, and embody what needs to be embodied at this moment of meta-crisis, so we can actually participate in the evolution of the source code.

And that takes a thousand *no*'s, my friends. It takes a thousand *no*'s in order to say the *Yes*.

There is a text from the third century, on the inside of the inside, the deepest of the deep, by Master Abbahu. He says that before this world was manifested (or created, or evolved, or however we tell that story), *Hakadosh Baruch Hu bara olamot bi'hishriban*, "God/Goddess created worlds, and then let them disappear and destroyed them."

There's this image of Infinity manifesting multiple worlds, and then destroying them, until Infinity chose *this* world. It is so deep. What the sacred text means is that **there are worlds we need to let go of, to allow them to crumble—in order to choose the world in which we need to live our story.**

We need to respond to the story of humanity at this moment in time.

We need to take our seat at the table of history and actually *act* to tell the new Story of Value.

It is only a new Story of Value that evolves the source code, that actually changes the fate, the direction, and the destiny of humanity.

That's why we say here every week that we are at this time between worlds; we are at this time between stories. It has to be clear and sharp—and it's so easy for it to get confused. It's got to be crystal clear. It's got to be completely sharp.

We are at this time between stories, at this time between worlds, just like they were in the Renaissance, when the old world order was breaking down, and a pandemic swept through Europe. Every time I say these words, they are new to me—and I've said them a thousand times. We are at a moment like the Renaissance but exponentially more critical. We are at the most critical moment that human history has ever known, from the perspective of existence. And we *can* step in.

It's not 100 years from now.

It's not fifty years now.

It's *right now*.

We *can* step in and tell this new Story of Value.

132

We *can* be that spiritual society, that band of Outrageous Lovers, and pour everything in and bring all the pieces together.

We don't try to just touch bases. So many of us have to-do lists, and we try to cover everything in the to-do list, but nothing gets done the way it should. Nothing embraces the fullness of our energy, where we sit on something and perfect it—we make it perfect, we make it beautiful. Rather, we move from activity to activity to activity, trying to get done as much as we can.

No!

Five *no*'s—say five *no*'s in order to say *Yes*.

That's what Divinity does.

That's what that sacred text is.

God says *no* to multiple worlds, to multiple universes, in order to say *Yes* to this possibility. The Big Bang is a *Yes!*—but in order to say that *Yes*, Infinity needed to say *no*. Infinity that has infinite power, infinite capacity, and infinite versatility. Infinity had to say *no*—not to everything, but to a lot, in order to say *Yes*.

And the first thing we do is, we say *Yes* to each other. Yes, yes, yes!

We are here together.

We are in Unique Self Symphony together. We each need each other in some profound way, and at the center of the center. We have to be pillars for each other, uniquely. And this is what God says to Goddess. This is what *Shiva* says to *Shakti*. This is what Earth says to Sky. This is what Krishna says to Radha: *I love you, I need you.*

Let's pour in and create this together.

Let's be so present together—because greatness is cumulative.

EROS IS THE PLACING OF ATTENTION

I want to just give you one more image. Have you all ever heard of something? And again, this may be new for people, I get it. But there's something that's called *sex*. I don't know if anyone's familiar with this. Anyone?

What is sex, at the very core? What is it?

At its very core, sex is the placing of attention. Sex means: I place my attention on you. The joy of sexuality isn't just in the titillation, the particular pleasure sensation which comes. The joy of sexuality is: *Oh my God, we're completely placing our attention on each other.* What sexuality is, at its core, is the placing of attention—when you are not looking at your watch, you are not texting (although people text and look at their watches today during sex all the time). You're in full focus.

You are doing what's called *simat lev* in Hebrew. The Hebrew word for the placing of attention is *simat lev*, "the placing of my heart." *Simat lev* means, "I've placed my heart on you."

I've placed my heart on you, and everything that flows from that is secondary.

Sometimes it might be agony, and sometimes it might be bliss.

Sometimes it might be tumultuous, and sometimes it might be spacious.

But **the reason we say that Reality is Eros, is because Eros is the placing of attention**. The sexual models the erotic. It *doesn't exhaust* the erotic, but the sexual models what it means to be in Eros.

In order to love Reality open at this moment in time, we need to make love to Reality.

I speak here from a place of fierce tenderness. To make love to Reality means *not* to self-pleasure. It's different than self-pleasuring—all blessings to masturbation, but that's not what it is. It's making love, and making love means I'm completely placing my attention on Reality and asking, *What do you need?*

That's what the lover does. The lover feels the need of the beloved, and the lover says to the beloved, *your need is my allurement*. Isn't that gorgeous? **Your need is my allurement.**

I can feel the way you need to be touched.

I can feel the exact intensity, firmness, softness, flutter, and pace—because we've completely placed our attention on each other.

In the lineage, we say, *Moshe*—Moses, that great figure of the Hebrew wisdom lineage—is *ish ha'Elohim*: he's the man, he's the groom, he's the prince—of the Divine, of the *Shekhinah*, of Reality itself. Moses is making love all the time. And then the *Zohar* says, in the thirteenth century, *et Moshe bekhol dara*, "Moses lives in each of us"—in every generation.

That's what it means to be in this band of Outrageous Lovers: to say, **what does Reality need from me in the very next moment?**

Not just my immediate circle—that's important, but it doesn't exhaust who I am if I am in a band of Outrageous Lovers.

Imagine it's 100 years from now, when actually all the things we've been talking about have manifested—because we didn't do what we needed to do!

To be Homo amor, to be the new human, to be the new humanity, is to have an experience that everything is in the balance, and my next decision tips everything over.

On the other hand, it's fully spacious and relaxed.

We celebrate. We are in joy, and we are not in the anxiety of the next moment.

It's the way of making love. It's the way of placing my attention to Reality, and then Reality loves me, and tenderly strokes my heart, kisses my soul, and loves me open in this dance.

This erotic dance begins between me and Reality, this dance of Amore.

That's our intention in Holy of Holies.

That's our intention in *One Mountain*, which is Holy of Holies.

That's our intention between each other.

That's our intention as a band of Outrageous Lovers.

Can everyone feel that? It's a unique call.

EVOLUTIONARY LOVE CODE: UNIQUE SELF ENCOUNTERS

Every true intimate encounter is a Unique Self encounter between soul stories.

In a true Unique Self encounter, we realize that we are all holding a piece of each other's story.

The ethical demand of a Unique Self encounter is that we return to each other the missing chapters of our stories.

The motive force of evolution is Unique Self encounters, in which we're constantly returning to each other the depth of our unique stories.

The ultimate expression of Reality is billions and billions of Unique Self encounters, which generate a Unique Self Symphony of stories, all of which are rooted in a shared Story of Value, as the ultimate context of our wild and sacred diversity.

A BREAKDOWN IN TRUST

There's an article that just appeared in *The Atlantic* magazine, called "America's Intimacy Problem." You might think, well, they've been at *One Mountain*; they are actually listening. There is an intimacy problem. It's a good intuition. It's a good start. But when you actually read the article, you get the challenge, the tragedy, the invitation, and the demand of this moment (and of course, you can replace *America* with *Europe* or *global*).

What the article essentially asks is, *Why are people non-intimate?* And it talks about how painful it is to watch just how disconnected people are. The article centers around an interview with Michael Hilgers, a well-known therapist on the American scene, and he explains it in terms of *attachment styles*.

Attachment styles are a particular form of psychological understanding that began about seventy years ago. Attachment theory basically says that the nature of your attachment with your early caretakers determines the trajectory of your life (by attachment, they mean love and trust, but attachment is a more neutral word). Will your life break down? Will it collapse? Will it fall apart? Will you be addicted? Will you be tormented? Or will you be able to live a stable life that is productive and satisfying, contributing to the whole, and filled with Goodness, Truth, and Beauty? Well, they say this is dependent on your early attachment.

But let's get *underneath* the words.

What attachment really means is: What's the love story?

What's the love story between you and your mother and father or between you and your early caretakers?

What's the love story that you experienced early in your life?

Because the universe is a love story, because we live in *The Universe: A Love Story*, because your early caretakers incarnate the universe—they *are* the universe—the way they hold you is your first experience of the love story.

The way we experience our first love story is how we're going to experience all of Reality—that's what attachment theory says. It doesn't use these words (if it did, it would be far more effective). It uses much more clinical words, but that's really what it means, even if attachment theorists don't fully acknowledge it. I've talked to any number of the key attachment theorists in the world and shared this with them, and they all said: *Yeah, that's actually right. We never would have said it that way, and we can't write about it in journals that way, we are afraid to. But yes, that's what it's about at its deepest core.*

There are four main styles of attachment:

- **Secure attachment** means you had a good attachment with the mother or father. In our language, it was a love story that worked, that you could feel at home in, that challenged you, that you were embraced in. Very few people have what's called secure attachment.

- Then there is what's called **avoidant attachment**. You desire attachment, but you avoid it. You insist on a certain kind of independence. You can't really listen. You can't really drop in. You can't fully surrender—whether it's to your family context or really to anything. You just can't do that ultimate step of surrender and deep love attachment. You may avoid it by being really busy and never really committing fully and all the way in any one place. You may avoid it by asserting your autonomy and your independence in ways that you don't need to.

- The third form is called **anxious attachment**. You want it, but you have a fear of it, which makes you very anxious, so you can't quite drop in.

- And then there is **disorganized attachment**, where you both want it and don't want it at the same time. It's confusing, and you're all over the map.

Avoidant attachment, anxious attachment, and disorganized attachment are based on one fundamental breakdown: a breakdown in trust. This article suggests that the world today is in a place of avoidant attachment, insecure attachment, or anxious attachment.

That's exactly what we've called here: *the global intimacy disorder.*

YOU CANNOT CREATE INTIMACY WITHOUT A SHARED STORY OF VALUE

The article diagnoses this collapse of trust based on exterior barometers, exterior ways of evaluating trust. But, it says, **the root causes of these trust issues are impossible to diagnose**.

- Maybe they are a reflection of America's worries about societal problems.
- In Europe, maybe it's the war.
- Maybe it's ChatGPT.
- Maybe it's financial insecurity. When society feels scary, maybe that seeps into your relationships.
- Others say that it's the smartphones—and certainly, smartphones have contributed something to the decline in physical intimacy, but smartphones don't quite account for it.
- Maybe it's that during Covid, people were apart from each other for long periods of time, and we haven't been able to reclaim intimacy.

In the end, the article says, **We don't know *why* people are putting up walls, growing further and further away from one another. We just know that it's happening.**

That's the tragedy of the article.

In the article, there's no real understanding of what intimacy is—just an understanding that intimacy breeds trust. But:

- ◆ We're not sure *how* to breed trust.
- ◆ We're not sure *why* it's falling apart.
- ◆ We're not sure why there's this collapse of trust, which is this collapse of intimacy.

Here's what they miss: **You cannot be intimate with someone, you cannot create intimacy, unless you are living in a shared story.**

You cannot even begin to address the global intimacy disorder, unless we are actually living in a shared Story of Value.

To the precise extent that a couple experiences themselves as being in a shared story, the couple creates intimacy.

- ◆ You can create intimacy at the role-mate level: we have shared roles, and we are in a shared story.
- ◆ You can create it at the soul-mate level: we're sharing the story of our vulnerability and our brokenness, our holy and broken *Hallelujah.*
- ◆ You can create it even more deeply at the whole-mate level because we're sharing the larger story together.

Intimacy means the depth of our shared story, and the more we *link* our shared story, the more we link our destiny by experiencing each other as being in a shared story of value, in which my story affects your story, and your story affects my story:

- ◆ We are not in a win/lose metrics.
- ◆ We are not each on our own individual hero's journey.
- ◆ We are not each involved on our own spiritual path (although that's also true—we are each Unique Selves with unique vocations and unique callings), but our Unique Selves are unique chapters of a *shared* story.

It's only the experience of a shared story that can address the intimacy disorder—and that shared story has to be a shared Story of Value, where we experience Reality itself as a Story of Value, in which value is real. Value is rooted in First Principles and First Values, which are intrinsic structures of Cosmos.

In other words, you cannot have intimacy unless we are in the Field of Value together, and to be in the Field of Value together means that we have a shared Story. A shared Story means we are in the Story of Value together.

MY LIFE IS AN OUTRAGEOUS LOVE STORY

We have talked extensively about Outrageous Love and ordinary love.

1. We live in a world of outrageous pain, and **the only response is Outrageous Love**. That was step one.

2. Outrageous Love is not ordinary love. It's not just a social construct. **Outrageous Love is the heart of existence itself**.

3. Outrageous Love lives personally, irreducibly, and uniquely, in each one of us. **We—each of us—are unique Outrageous Lovers**.

4. Therefore, what's there to do? **Commit Outrageous Acts of Love**.

5. Which Outrageous Acts of Love? **Those that are a function of your Unique Self**.

6. How do you arouse that experience of Outrageous Love, which is almost impossible to hold? **You arouse this experience by writing Outrageous Love Letters**, by writing Outrageous Love Notes. By writing Outrageous Love Notes, you enter into the Field of Outrageous Love, and you arouse the actual first-person experience. And you realize *who am I?* **I'm an Outrageous Lover writing Outrageous Love Letters**.

7. Then you ask, *Who am I?* **I realize that *I am* an Outrageous Love Letter**. My Unique Self is God's/Goddess's Outrageous

Love Letter to me, and **my Outrageous Acts of Love are my Outrageous Love Letter back to the Infinity of Intimacy,** back to Reality, back to the Divine, back to the globe that desperately needs my Outrageous Acts of Love.

This all means that **I begin to conceive my life as an Outrageous Love Story.**

I realize that my life is not ordinary.

My life is extraordinary because my life is an Outrageous Love Story. It's a unique love story, which is chapter and verse in *The Universe: A Love Story*, and the plotline of my life is my Outrageous Love Story. It includes my romantic loves, my Outrageous Lover, my Outrageous Acts of Love, my Outrageous Love Letters, and my outrageous erotic love letters. It includes the unique configuration of intimacy and Eros, which is my life.

My life is an Outrageous Love Story, and it participates in the Outrageous Love Story of Reality.

There is this article on intimacy in a major Western magazine—and they don't know what intimacy is, so they can only identify it by its lack. They say the collapse of intimacy is identifiable because there is a lack of trust. Then they say, we don't know why. We can only tell you that the collapse is there, but there is no way to understand why.

They offer all sorts of possibilities. Maybe it's the global crisis, so we're afraid to love each other. They don't quite say it that way, but the fear gets in the way of intimacy, maybe. Maybe it's smartphones. Maybe it's the pandemic.

But no—all of those are symptoms. Those are all important, but those are symptoms.

What's *the root cause* of the global intimacy disorder?

Does everyone begin to get why this new Story of Value we're telling *matters*? Because **if you cannot diagnose, you cannot heal**. And telling the new Story of Value is first a diagnostic.

- We have to diagnose.
- We have to accurately see the breakdown.
- From that accurate seeing of the breakdown comes the breakthrough.

You need to understand the nature of the emergency, and from that comes the new emergence.

That's what it means when we say, *Our crisis is a birth.*

Crisis is an evolutionary driver only if I understand that every crisis is a crisis of intimacy.

But what is intimacy?

Intimacy means we live in a shared story—but not an ordinary shared Story, an Outrageous Love Story as a Story of Value: we live in a shared story of intrinsic value, and we experience ourselves in the Field of Value together.

We feel each other in the Field of Value, and then we begin to resonate with each other. In our own unique circles of intimacy and influence, we resonate with each other; we become intimate with each other.

WE ARE HOLDING PIECES OF EACH OTHER'S STORIES

I want, in the light of that, to read a piece from the evolutionary love code again: ***Every true intimate encounter is a Unique Self encounter between soul stories. In a true Unique Self encounter, we realize that we're all holding a piece of each other's story.***

143

When God meets Goddess, when Krishna meets Radha, when the *Shekhinah* meets *tiferet*, when the upper waters meet the lower waters, when Earth meets Sky, when line meets circle—when that *really* happens, we understand: *Oh my God, I love you, I need you.*

- I need you desperately.
- I love you desperately.
- My desperation is ecstatic, filled with joy.

We come to understand that we are holding a piece of each other's story—and the most pressing ethical demand of our life, which is the ethical demand of a Unique Self encounter, is that we return to each other the missing pieces of our stories.

We are each holding a piece of each other's story.

To be in an Outrageous Love Story is to know:

- I have Outrageous Lovers, who are my beloveds.
- Those Outrageous Lovers who are in my unique circle of empathy and influence—Reality has placed them close to me. Reality has worked hard to bring us together because we have a piece of each other's story.
- The motive force of evolution is Unique Self encounters, in which we return to each other the missing pieces of our story.

Wow! Can you feel that? Can you feel the resonance in that? That is what intimacy means.

Intimacy means we have shared identity, in the sense that we are part of a shared story of value.

We are unique expressions. We each have unique stories.

We each have Unique Self stories in Unique Self Symphony—**our stories resonate with each other, they evoke something.**

We realize my story is not *just* my story. I'm not just living my spiritual path or my hero's journey. In my story, there's a piece of your story, and there's something that happens when we are together that allows me to return to you a piece of your story and allows you to return to me a piece of my story.

That's intimacy, and that's what trust means:

I'm going to return to you a piece of your story, by being radically present and radically on the inside with you, promising you I'll be here forever.

We've got to be here forever for each other. That's what evolutionary family means. The nature of biological family is that we know we are forever—but we think evolutionary family is just a little moment, a little episode we had in our lives.

No, **evolutionary family has to be forever**. Every intimate encounter that's real is forever.

One of the principles that I teach in sexuality is that there should never be sexuality between two people who are not going to love each other forever. That love may express in many different forms—but you have to love each other forever. And it's not just sexual intimacy—the sexual models the erotic. In a true intimate encounter, when we have a piece of each other's story, we look in each other's eyes, and we say it's forever.

+ I'm going to be returning your story to you every single day.
+ I'm never *not* going to return your story to you.

That's a Unique Self Symphony.

That's the beginning of the healing of a global intimacy disorder:

1. We live in a shared Story of Value.

2. We are each unique expressions of that shared Story of Value.
3. That shared story of value means that in our unique stories, we have not only our own story but a piece of our beloved's story—and by being in each other's presence, we evoke something in each other that no one else can evoke—by talking to each other, by being in each other's presence, by sharing in the space.

There are many different levels:

*   Sometimes, we evoke this just by *being* in each other's presence.
*   Other times, we do it through *deep study*.
*   Other times, we do it by *creating together*.

But we are radically focused; we've placed our attention on each other.

We're making love in every second—and we're making love *forever*.

ARE WE WILLING TO LOVE EACH OTHER DESPERATELY?

To be in a spiritual society, in a band of Outrageous Lovers, means that we have stepped in together, that we are going to place our attention on each other, and that we are not going to look away. Sometimes we have to come closer, and sometimes we need to step back in order to attend to other things that need attention.

But then we step back in. **We never look away.**

And we realize: Oh my God, here we are in 2023. We've been placed in this moment. We've done that exercise my friend suggested to me, where we come back to this moment in time 100 years from now, and we can make choices now.

We can make choices to love each other more madly than ever before.

We can make choices to focus and to say a thousand *no*'s in order to scream the *Yes* of the ultimate explosion—into union and into rapture.

There is steadiness, a placing of attention, and a placing of the heart. Wow!

I want to invite you to do another exercise, which has two steps. It's a beautiful, stunning exercise:

- First, we ask: **Are we willing to love each other *desperately*?** You can only love desperately when you realize that in every *I love you*, there is *I need you*. Am I willing to love you desperately and to need you desperately? That's one.
- Second, we ask: **Am I willing to realize that I have a piece of your story that's mine to return to you?** To actually know that I need you, that I cannot do it without you?

You might think I can. You think it's just technical and functional, and you think I can keep showing up. But I cannot. I cannot. There is something that you pour into me, something that I pour into you, that no one that ever was, is, or will be can pour. Wow!

She places us next to each other.

She says, love each other madly, be a band of Outrageous Lovers, and know that each of you has a piece of each other's story:

- Without which you can't be whole.
- Without which you can't be an Outrageous Lover.
- Without which we can't be in an Outrageous Love Story together.
- Without which we cannot participate in evolving the source code of culture and consciousness in telling this new Story of Value in response to this meta-crisis, in response to this breakdown.

It's so real, my friends. It's so real, and it's so beautiful.

And so, we have to *speak of each other's love in the morning, and trust each other through the night,* and trust that we're always there for each other. That's what Solomon said.

Friends, if I was too fierce today, I'm only talking to myself. I'm just talking out loud to myself, I am just inviting myself—and thank you for listening in. If you feel that it speaks to you in any small way, then I'm madly honored.

We're at a crossroads, and it's ours to do. Here I place my love for you.

CHAPTER TWELVE

THE SACRED IS THE INTIMATE: RESPONDING TO THE META-CRISIS THROUGH THE EVOLUTION OF INTIMACY

Episode 376 — December 21, 2023

TO BE SACRED IS TO BE INTIMATE

Wow, it's Christmas! Merry Christmas, everyone. Merry Christmas! What a moment to do Christmas in. I'd like to really be with you in *the depth* of Christmas.

What is Christmas?

What is the unique contribution of this Christmas moment to Reality?

What is the Christ?

What are we here to do together? What is One Mountain, Many Paths?

We are here not only to comfort, but also to comfort. **We want to comfort the afflicted. But we also want to afflict the comfortable.** We want to stand clearly and be in the sacred.

I want to begin by making an offering, and it's a very, very, very profound offering. It's profound, not because I'm making it but because it reaches deep, deep into the lineages of the Christ, to make a very fundamental offering.

The offering is: Jesus is the Christ. The Christ is the Holy One, the Sacred One.

To be sacred is to be intimate.

That's the sentence: to be sacred is to be intimate.

I've been reading intensely the scholarship of Christianity through the night. About six weeks ago, I spent maybe four hours until five in the morning, deep in the texts and in the scholarship of the word *Kadosh*, meaning "holy" or "sacred."

The basic movement in much of scholarship, based on reading a multitude of texts, is that *the sacred* means *transcendent*. Rudolf Otto talks about the sacred in that way, as does Nachmanides in the classical Hebrew tradition, as does Rashi, one of the great exegetes of the sacred texts. And, of course, they're saying something important. What they mean is that **the sacred is not reducible to categories of social construction.**

The sacred is more than psychology that is constructed, or made up, out of a reductive materialist condition, in which the human being arises by accident in a random and pointless cosmos. That's what they mean by that—that the sacred is an entire other order of being.

But ultimately, they lead us astray.

Those of us who've been together for many years understand, I hope, that I say that with a lot of trembling and trepidation and not with a casual or superficial recklessness or audacity. I think that's a wrong reading of the text. I hope this year we will be able to do four hours on a reading of the word "sacred" in the biblical text—what does that word actually mean throughout the corpus of the text?

I think that what you will see is, based on a very close reading of that text, that to be sacred is to be intimate. There is only one other scholar that I've seen who aligns with me on this, and I believe that he's correct. His name is Eliezer Berkovits. He wrote a book that was published by Wayne State University Press. It's out of print. When he died, I went to his apartment in Jerusalem and found a couple of copies left of his old book.

He does this remarkable study, dozens and dozens of pages, into the idea of the word "holy". I'm just going to read to you the last three sentences:

"Rather than the holy indicating transcendence, it seems, based on a careful reading of the texts, to be inseparable from the idea of immanence." (*Immanence* is not transcendence, not *the other*, but immanent, close, inherent.) "Far from meaning inaccessibility, it reveals closeness and association."

And then Berkovits concludes, in contradistinction to Rudolf Otto: "It's not the *mysterium tremendum*. If anything, it is its very opposite."

The *mysterium tremendum* means the other, the transcendent.

I read you the last three lines of the article because I want to ground us in this deep understanding that I've tried to develop in my own teaching and that Berkovits has developed in his teaching. I want to, at some point, bring them together in a full study, and it'll be a key part of our understanding of *The Universe: A Love Story*.

THE MYSTERY OF THE CHRIST IS THAT GOD IS THE INFINITE INTIMATE

But enough now of the scholarly apparatus, let me just get to the point.

The *mysterium tremendum* means there is mystery between us, and that's beautiful. That's a dimension of love. But **the sacred appears when the mystery discloses itself—**

- ◆ and we can touch each other,
- ◆ and we can feel each other,
- ◆ and we can hold each other in profound intimacy.

To be sacred, in the closest reading of the deepest strains of the texts, means to be intimate.

This is why, for example in Leviticus 19, when it says *ve'atim k'doshim, ki kadosh Ani,* "you shall be sacred, for I am sacred," it then launches into a set of texts about interpersonal relations, which climax in *ve'ahavta l're'akha kamokh,* "love each other madly." **Love your beloved as you love yourself.** Love them madly. *Ani Adonai,* "because I am the Divine, and I am sacred."

To be sacred means to love madly—but to love madly means to be intimate.

That is the realization of the Christ.

The realization of the Christ is that Infinity—which is ultimately transcendent, ultimately other, which is *mysterium tremendum,* full mystery—the mystery says:

> Feel me. I want you to feel me, I am in search of you. I need you to feel me. I am the Infinite, and yet I have a need, and that need is to be intimate with you.
>
> And in my intimacy with you, I become more infinite.
>
> In my intimacy with you, I become more whole.
>
> When *you* reach out of yourself, and you feel me, I become more me.
>
> And when *I* reach out of my *mysterium tremendum* and I feel you, I become more me.

When the human being is in search of *She,*

- when we bracket the vagaries of the supercilious ego, grasping and seeking,
- and we feel Divinity on the inside,
- we feel the pulsing of *Her* joy,

- we feel the throbbing of *Her* desire,
- we feel the infinity of *Her* pain—

—then we become more human.

When Divinity, *Deus Absconditus,* "the hidden God," reaches out of the Heavens, reaches from the depths—

- and discloses *Her* heart for but a moment,
- and we feel *Her* heart, and we feel its pulsing, and we feel its joy, and we feel *Her* yearning,
- when *She* reaches out of the infinite, and *She* feels our heart,
- and *She* feels our pain, and *She* feels our joy,
- when *She*'s intimate with us—

—*She* becomes more *She*. *She* becomes more whole. *She* becomes more God.

Christ means: **I feel you so deeply that, in some sense, I *become* you**.

That's what we are afraid to do.

We are afraid to feel each other so deeply that we become each other because we're afraid that we're going to lose ourselves. But the mystery of the Christ is that **when I feel you so deeply and lose myself inside of you, only then am I found for the very first time**.

That's the mystery of the Christ.

The mystery of the Christ is that I can empty myself out and fill myself with you, and then I become more filled with my selfhood than I ever was. That's the mystery of the Christ.

The mystery of the Christ is that God is the Infinite Intimate. God is the infinite other who is *mysterium tremendum,* who desires—more than anything—to intimately touch the deepest recess, the deepest shards of our holy and broken *Hallelujahs*.

It's so deep. It's so deep. It's so deep.

THE DEMONIC IS THE FAILURE OF INTIMACY

As we moved from premodernity to modernity, we understood that we needed to introduce universal human rights. We said that not just the king has rights, not just the court or the royalty, but every human being has a right to life and a right to the dignity of their individuated personhood.

That was an expression of this movement, this evolution of love, this evolution of consciousness—this fundamental set of rights that protect us against incursion from the outside by the forces of empire, in all of her distressing disguises.

That was a critical set of rights.

Modernity was defined by this demand for rights and this democratization of rights, which is beautiful.

Postmodernity said, "Let's expand those rights to those who are marginalized, to those who are on the corners, the edges of society— whether it be sexual alternatives or dimensions of appropriate gender alternatives, in ways that are sane and good, or marginalized populations whose stories may have been overridden or rewritten by the victors and the vagaries of history."

That impulse, per se, was a sacred impulse: let's expand the rights that modernity claimed. But in that claiming of rights—in the sacred claiming of rights—there was this hyper-autonomy, this hyper-individuation. It was about the rights of the nation and the rights of the individual. It was beautiful. **But it was autonomy that lost its relationship to its beloved: communion—intimate communion.**

And so we created a world of rivalrous conflict governed by win/lose metrics, the first generator function of the meta-crisis of existential risk. This generated complicated systems in which the pieces and parts didn't know each other.

We've talked about that many times here.

And in the text that is the gateway to One Mountain Many Paths, *Love or Die*, we unpack that matrix of our conversation. **All of this together, all of this assertion of rights, beautiful as it was, left us alone**, left us in our silos, left us hollow and stuffed—the hollow men, the stuffed men. It left us as desiccated Giacometti sculptures, denuded from the larger fields of intimacy—generating a global intimacy disorder, which is at the heart of the meta-crisis.

For example, in Israel, as we've been wrenched in pain in Israel and Gaza, we have to madly feel, more intimately than ever before, the horror and the pain of the innocent civilians dying under rubble in Gaza—even as we need to draw the obvious bright line between a culture of jihad, which is a culture of death, and a Western pluralistic democracy, which is radically committed to honoring life.

There is a reason why every Arab leader is still privately calling Israel and saying, if Hamas is allowed to continue, we will have millions of deaths; there's a reason why that's happening. It is a bright distinction, a bright moral line. If you can't draw that moral line, you can't draw any moral lines.

But even as we draw that moral line, we can never be so lost in that which is right—even as we're absorbed in the rightness of what the necessary response is for the sake of goodness, truth, and beauty, and for the sake of having a world that doesn't collapse in and on itself—nonetheless, we have to be intimate.

I have two text threads on my phone. And every single day, I receive the faces of boys, often friends of people that I know, who have been killed in battle. Twelve in the last two days.

My son just wrote me a text this morning saying: *Dad, I'm back in reserve duty,* meaning *I was called back.* The implication: active duty, and *I won't be available for a little while.* And even then, I've got to look at the other text thread, and I have to see the faces.

Not just numbers—the faces of innocent men, women, and children, who have been killed, as innocent German men, women, and children were killed, in the bombing of Germany to defeat Nazism. I have to feel their pain.

And even more—I have to feel the pain of the guilty as well. Even the guilty, I can't other. Even the guilty, I can't so utterly demonize that I don't feel their pain—or I become a demon. **The demonic is the failure of intimacy**. That's the nature of the demonic. The demonic is non-intimate. Christ is intimate. The Christ is intimate.

LET US BE INTIMATE WITH THE CHRIST

If you can, for a second, close your eyes. I just want to meditate with you for a moment. Let's just be in the words for a second.

Today is Christmas.

It's Christmas Eve.

And let us be intimate with the Christ.

Let us be intimate first with Mary. Let's be Mary's body, all of us.

We are all Mary, and our bodies are pregnant. Life is growing in our belly, the life of the Divine.

The infinite Christ, that which is waiting to be birthed through me. The new god that's not going to be born in the public spaces of social media, but the new god that's going to be born in the silent humility, the tenderness of the private manger, my body.

My body is the place in which a unique Christ, a unique gift can be born.

We are all the mother, and we are all the baby.

We are all the Christ.

We are the Infinite becoming the baby, and the Infinite embracing new innocence, born into this veil of tears, this world of agony and ecstasy, this world of mystery.

And we are all John the Baptist, longing for the wilderness, reaching for devotion, for desire, reaching to baptize our hearts in water and fire.

And we are all Magdalene. We are all the dignity of desire, transformed into the torrential tenderness of the torn heart, and the gorgeousness of touch, which is *She* incarnate.

And we are also Pilate and his confusion, and Herod and his raging ego and murderous fear.

And we are also caught in the crowds of social media that are willing to offer up the Christ in return for a few likes.

And we are all death, and we are all resurrection.

It's all of us, my friends. It's all of us.

We are celebrating Christmas here, as family.

To be family to each other means:

- that we feel each other,
- that we are creating a new structure of intimacy in the world,
- that intimacy is not only biological family, where we are immanent by the decision of biology, and where intimacy often gets distorted and becomes long years of therapy, to try to understand the relationships in the family, desperate for some understanding and some mutual empathy.

And blessings to family, and blessings to biological family, which is so sacred and so important, because it's the decision of *She* to bring this particular group of people together.

But *She* speaks in a second voice, and the second voice is the voice of *Evolutionary Family*.

Barbara Marx Hubbard, we celebrate you today.

We are intimate with you in the continuity of consciousness, my beloved evolutionary whole mate.

We celebrate you. We feel you, and you feel us.

We talk together about this new vision of evolutionary intimacy that you held so dear, and that we held so dear together, and we invoke evolutionary family.

Barbara, for the last five years of your life—and, as you related to me, for most of your life—your evolutionary family was the core, the place where you felt and were felt, the place where you lived and breathed.

Let's invoke evolutionary family, which means that in *One Mountain*, we love each other, we feel each other, we hold each other.

We are an engine of revolution.

But that engine is not simply the infrastructures of funding, as critical as they are.

And it's not the infrastructures of operations, as critical as they are.

But at the very core of this revolution called *One Mountain*—which seeks to respond to the meta-crisis, the global intimacy disorder, with a new Story of Value—is the intimacy between us.

It's imperfect.

It's all holy and broken; we are making mistakes, but we're making mistakes in the right direction.

We love each other.

We care for each other.

We feel each other.

We become the Christ by being willing to feel each other.

EVOLUTIONARY LOVE CODE: FROM BIOLOGICAL TO EVOLUTIONARY FAMILY

Biological family is one, and we are committed to it. Evolutionary family or soul root family is not less, and sometimes even more significant.

We need to be, at the very least, as committed to our evolutionary family, as we are to our biological family, and often much more so.

It is before your evolutionary family that you can confess your greatness, take your unique risk, speak and live your deepest heart's desire, and be seen in the depth of your true glory.

We will not be able to respond to existential risk without making the momentous leap from only biological family, to biological family and evolutionary or soul root family.

THERE IS A RIGHT TO INTIMACY

Evolutionary family means that we all have the right to family.

Everyone has a right to family.

Some people get what seems to be great families, but lots of people don't. Everyone has a right to a great family, but **the right to a great family is part of a larger new right**.

We said that modernity and postmodernity were about classical human rights, the rights to be protected against incursion from the outside. But all of that together, we said, generated this global intimacy disorder, which generated the roots of the meta-crisis.

We need to create a new structure of intimacy.

We need to create evolutionary intimacy. And we need to speak up about **the right to intimacy**.

There's a book that we talked about, about a year and a half ago. It's by Amia Srinivasan at Oxford, and it's called *The Right to Sex*, in which, essentially, she's mocking the idea that someone would have the right to sex, or the right to desire, and she associates it with incel communities.

First off, mad blessings to Amia, and Merry Christmas to you, with much love and honor.

But she misses the point.

The sexual *models* Eros. It doesn't exhaust Eros. It's not about sex. It's all about sex, and it's not about sex at all. Sex is an expression, one expression of something much deeper, which is the Field of Eros. And the Field of Eros is the Field of Intimacy, the Intimate Universe. There actually *is* a right to intimacy.

Eros has two dimensions—desire and intimacy.

- We have a right to desire and to be desired, and we have a right to be intimate.
- We have a right to be intimate with ourselves.
- We have a right to be intimate with each other one-on-one, as beloveds.
- We have a right to be intimate with a circle of beloveds, which is our evolutionary family.

Those are fundamental human rights.

We have a right to be intimate with a larger intimate communion with the world. Not just with our evolutionary family, but to be intimate with the whole, to be omni-considerate for the sake of the whole, to feel the whole.

We have a right to feel the whole.

We have a right to feel the Field of Intimacy, the Field of Value, which is *the Tao*.

Those are fundamental human rights. But *not only* are they rights. **A right is also a need**. At their core, there is no distinction between a right and a need. **My most fundamental clarified needs are my rights.**

- If I need intimacy in order to survive, then I have a right to intimacy.
- If I need water in order to live, I have a right to water.
- If I need air, I have a right to air.
- If I need basic income to survive, then I may have a right to universal basic income.

My core needs are my core rights.

It turns out that **my most clarified needs are also my deepest heart's desires**. My most clarified need is not just the need to survive. It's not just a need to be close. It's not just a need to be warm. Although, it is all of those, and every human being in the world has those basic rights.

But I also have a need to be held, touched, and received; I have a need to find my goodness in the face of the other and to be surrounded by an evolutionary family that loves me.

Those are also my deepest heart's desires.

I have a need to be intimate with my irreducible uniqueness and give my unique gift.

I have a need to realize that I'm not just separate self. Intimacy at the level of separate self is often a negotiation between two people, to try to have at least basic lines of communication and to take care of each other. But all too often, between separate selves, it's very hard to create intimacy.

I need to move beyond my separate self, which is often in a state of war and a perpetual power struggle, and I need to access my True Self, which is the

Field of Oneness, the Field of Desire, the Field of Intimacy, and the Field of Value.

Then the entire Field is intimate, which is why Dogen said, the Field is enlightenment, which is intimacy with all things. Everything is in the Field. Everything is alive, shimmering in *shunyata*.

But then the Field is disclosed as irreducible expressions of uniqueness, and I am irreducibly unique. I need to be intimate with my own unique gift, which then allows me to receive *your* unique gift, to see you, and to be intimate with your unique gift.

Then I need to be intimate with the unique personal pulsing of evolution alive in me, the evolutionary impulse, which is my evolutionary Unique Self, which then allows me to join the Unique Self Symphony in the ultimate intimacy of music, as we're each playing our own instrument together, in response to the global intimacy disorder.

There is a right to intimacy.

Intimacy is my most fundamental need.
Intimacy is my deepest heart's desire.

And intimacy is the quality of the sacred, and the Christ is the intimate one. Christ means that the infinite power of all of Reality desperately needs and desires and has a divine right to be intimate, and therefore a divine right to manifest and to create you and me and we, and she and he, and thee. Wow.

INTIMACY IS FOREVER: CELEBRATING BARBARA MARX HUBBARD

I want to celebrate Barbara, and then we're going to end in a couple of chants and prayers. But I really want to—just if we can—*receive* Barbara, who founded this *One Mountain* with us, who is with us every week, who

I miss intensely and dearly all the time, and I know we all do. With great, great love and great, great honor, for our beloved Barbara Marx Hubbard.

Did Barbara disappear? Does Barbara not exist? Did she move from that place of intensification of presence, and now she is gone, she has disappeared?

If you can actually find it in your body, it's obvious that that's not the case. When you can intimately feel someone's presence, when you are in the depth of intimacy with the beloved other, you understand that **intimacy is forever**, and you get this feeling—that's really clear, good, and obvious— that we'll all be together again.

Intimacy invokes eternity.

Intimacy tells me that *forever* is true.

Intimacy tells me that all the injustices will be made just, all the unfairnesses will become fair, all the broken hearts will be healed, and all the ruptured bodies will taste rapture.

That's what intimacy tells me. Intimacy tells me that the broken and the holy are the same—and if we are close, if we are intimate, then it all comes together again.

But feel it not in your mind; let your mind go if you can, beloveds. Let your mind go for a second.

The mind is beautiful, and I love the mind. But this is beneath and beyond the mind. This is the ultimate intimacy.

When we look in each other's eyes, and you just know, death is not the end; there's a continuity of consciousness. Because **if death were the end, then Reality would be ultimately non-intimate**. Feel our Barbara, feel her presence, feel her intimately, and know the truth—the intimate truth of the continuity of consciousness—on this silent night, this holy night.

SILENT NIGHT, HOLY NIGHT

We are going to conclude with three chants.

Stay with us for just a few more minutes. Be with us on the inside. Try—tenderly, tenderly—not to *consume*: *I got the ideas, now I'm gone.*

Let us be in the intimacy together, and actually be home together. We're going to do three chants, and we're just going to do a short thirty-second meditation between them.

Silent night, holy night. To be holy is to be intimate, and to be intimate is to be the Christ. And we're the Christ, and we're John the Baptist, and we're Mary, and we're Magdalene, and we're Herod, and we're Pilate, and we're the crowd.

Silent night, holy night.

Holy night means intimate night, and *intimacy* means I feel you.

I bracket myself, and I feel you, and you bracket yourself, and you feel me. And I feel you feeling me. You feel me feeling you. And **in that moment of being felt, loneliness disappears, and the gates of blessing are opened**. That's why we can't go demonic when we're intimate. We only go demonic when we erase the features of the face of the enemy, and we see only our own dead and not the dead of our beloveds. Justice is sometimes necessary. But in the end, as Gandhi said correctly, if it remains forever an eye for an eye, we all go blind. It doesn't mean justice disappears. Justice is necessary, or unbearable suffering destroys the globe.

Even when justice is necessary, when you read the sacred texts, you realize that, in the inner texts of the interior science, the Angel of Death is the lover, which is why love and death are so related. It's why the orgasm is: *Come my darling*, writes John Donne, *that I may die with you. Come, my darling, that I may die with you.*

To be intimate is to be gathered up in the arms of the beloved who protects me and holds me.

We just have two more steps in our practice of intimacy. And we're in practice now, we're on the inside of the inside. We are the Christ. Now, let's just feel John and Yoko, my dear friends. And what it means to be the Christ is: *I can feel it all.* I feel the joy, and I can feel it all.

Let us just, for a moment, my friends, bracket self. Let us feel it all.

And we'll go the very last step, my friends.

We are Christmas together. We are *Homo amor* together.

Homo amor is the Christ.

Homo amor is the atheist who says, "It's only me, and therefore, I feel it all and all value lives in me," which is the atheist who is the heretic but the heretic who's so filled with faith.

And all the distinctions and labels disappear, and it's the intimacy that lives in our hearts that is the sacred pulse beating, in which we know that it all matters, and it's all precious and all sacred. And every breath and move we make is held in the arms of *She*, and every place we fall, we fall into Her hands.

We are just going to read the last set of words, and then we're going to finish with that chant, *In Excelsis Deo*, with this we began and with this we end.

> *Angels we have heard on high.*
> *Sweetly singing o'er the plains.*
> *And the mountains in reply,*
> *Echoing their joyous strains.*
> *Gloria, in Excelsis Deo!*
> *Shepherds, why this jubilee?*
> *Why your joyous strains prolong?*
> *What the gladsome tidings be?*
> *Which inspire your heavenly song?*

We see Him in a manger laid,
Whom the choirs of angels praise.
Mary, Joseph, lend your aid.
While our hearts in love we raise.
Come to Bethlehem and see
Him Whose birthday angels sing.
Come, adore on bended knee
Christ the Lord, the newborn King.

Ultimate intimacy.

- And we need Rumi.
- And we need the radical atheist, who's the materialist mystic, who's the heretic who's filled with faith.
- And we need the mystical spark, the sacred intimate spark of Christendom.
- And we need the Islamic mystics.
- And we need Confucius.
- And we need Indigenous wisdom.

We need the sacred sparks and their unique expressions to write, tell, and be this new Story of Value.

My friend wrote to me this week, my beloved; she wrote, *when we tell the story of Unique Self, when we tell the story of Evolutionary Unique Self, when we tell the story of Homo amor, then we recognize ourselves.*

We tell a story, we write a poem, we write a sonnet—to recognize, most intimately, our deepest and truest nature. To Christ, to intimacy, to The Sacred, we sing.

Mad, mad, mad, Merry Christmas, my friends. Literally—without grandiosity, with trembling intimacy—we are responsible for it in this generation.

It's ours to do.

Just ours? It's never just ours. Everyone should do what they need to do.

But—

- ◆ writing this new Story of Value,
- ◆ telling this new story, knowing this Story,
- ◆ articulating this Great Library,
- ◆ writing sacred texts for the intimate communions of the future,
- ◆ responding to the global intimacy disorder with a new Story of Value, rooted in First Values and First Principles, a shared grammar of value as a context for our diversity—

—that's intimacy. It's only shared value that creates intimacy. In Excelsis Deo, Glory! Christ the Savior. Christ the Savior was born in this moment. So take us inside all the way, Bocelli. Thank you, Bocelli!

Oh my God, Merry Christmas! Merry Christmas! Merry Christmas!

We're it, man! This is the revolution. This is us. Oh my God. What a crazy, crazy delight. What a crazy delight! It doesn't get better. Merry Christmas, everyone, from all over the world.

CHAPTER THIRTEEN

THE EVOLUTION OF THE STUDENT-TEACHER RELATIONSHIP

Episode 386 — March 14, 2024

EVOLVING THE SOURCE CODE OF CONSCIOUSNESS AND CULTURE

We are at this moment, in this time between worlds and time between stories, when in order to reconfigure Reality, we need to participate in what I have called, for the last fifteen years, *evolving the source code of consciousness and culture.*

I remember when I first shared this with Tami Simon, who runs a company called Sounds True. I was talking about this idea of evolving the source code, and there was a very sharp pushback against this notion. It was a pushback against the notion that there *is* a source code because **a *source code* means there is something *immutable*.** However:

There is something immutable.

There is something eternal.

There is something that's unchanging—and we can also *evolve* that unchanging thing.

We can change and deepen that which is unchanging—and it will remain eternal and yet evolve.

It is a moment of either revolution or death.[2] If you look carefully at a good meta-analysis of the state of the world today, which we are doing together with our partners, you'll see that we are facing *the second shock of existence.*

The first shock of existence at the dawn of human history was the realization that death is an inevitable part of human existence. Death is a door between two days, but it *is* part of human existence.

Then, we go through all the stages of human history and get to the second shock of existence, which is the more recent realization of not *personal* mortality but *collective* mortality—the potential death of humanity itself. We can call it *existential risk,* or *the meta-crisis.*

There is a viable and real possibility that humanity as we know it will, over the next decades or hundreds of years, actually cease to exist. There will be another extinction. There have already been six mass extinction events for various reasons, but this one will be generated by the exponential power of technology, unmoored from wisdom, unmoored from the Field of Value, unmoored from the interior sciences—this radical split between interiors and exteriors at the very fabric of existence.

How many of you have heard me say this before? Pretty much everyone.

But we have to recontextualize and locate ourselves every week because it's very easy to look away, so I say it again, in one form or another, every week—in order to locate myself, to locate us, to orient the compass of the revolution.

What are we doing?

---

2   See *Love or Die: First Notes on Eros—Early Meditations on CosmoErotic Humanism* (World Philosophy and Religion Press, 2024).

This is not a Jesus church. This is not a little mystery church for nice and beautiful spiritual experiences. That's not what this is. There are places for that:

- There is a place for Jesus.
- There is a place for the Christ.
- There is a place for *Atman is Brahman*.
- There is a place for *Ma'at*, a place for *Geist*, and a place for *Adonai Hu Ha Elohim*.

There is a place for modern versions of all the old religions. But that's not what we are doing. **Today we are attuning to the essential allurement of Cosmos today.**

The essential allurement of Cosmos is this desperate need for a new Story of Value that responds to the second shock of existence and allows us to navigate that second shock—**a new Story of Value that can walk us through this eleventh hour of human existence, through this time between worlds.**

We need a new Story of Value that emerges in this time between stories and actually changes the game.

We always refer back to the Renaissance because the Renaissance was also a time between worlds and a time between stories—between the premodern political, economic, social, religious world, and what was going to emerge as the modern world. While most of Florence—there were nine other families in Florence besides the Medici—was concerned with the complexities of Florentine politics, Ficino, da Vinci, and the whole gang were able to see around the corner, and they began to tell a new Story of Value, which birthed modernity:

- To the extent that they got the plotlines right, they birthed what Habermas called *the dignities* of modernity.
- To the extent that the plotlines were lost, *the disasters* of modernity became the causative forces of existential risk.

SOCIAL SYNERGY IS NOT ENOUGH

My dear friend and evolutionary whole mate, beloved Barbara Marx Hubbard, was teaching about win/lose metrics as a core generator function of existential risk.

She didn't *call it* a generator function. My dear friend, Daniel Schmachtenberger, uses this term. But Daniel and I were deeply impacted by Barbara. Barbara deeply got this win/lose dimension. It was the insight that she ran with—that **these win/lose metrics are at the core of everything**.

Let us now add to that. **The win/lose metric stands against "social synergy."** Social synergy means that we can identify what's already working worldwide and bring it together. That was Barbara's understanding, that we need to generate social synergy—without that, we're going to collapse because our systems are complicated (rather than complex) and therefore fragile.

When Barbara and I met, she had already articulated this notion of win/lose metrics, and this notion of social synergy, which would stand against complicated systems. Daniel, Barbara, and I sat down and did a deep talk on the future human. Barbara had laid that ground down, but it didn't quite work. It was important and true but partial. Then Barbara and I started studying.

She did what was called Holy of Holies with me, which is this deep process of interior study, where we go into the source code. Barbara was more delighted, more open, more alive, more curious, more filled with audacity and humility than any eighty-three-year-old that I've ever seen. We spent five years in deep study, where I began to talk about intimacy, value, Eros, and the Field of Value.

Social synergy is not enough. Barbara lived in this world of techno-optimism. My friend Ken Wilber was also originally a techno-optimist, but he later shifted his course very dramatically and beautifully. Originally all of us were techno-optimists in some sense. We once believed in the social potential of the internet.

- But in the end, it doesn't hold.
- In the end, it breaks down.
- In the end, the internet is generating a Skinner box, which seeks to control us with invisible technologies and is tightening its vise around the way we think, breathe, and feel.

If you think that's not true, take a look at a ten-year-old. Take a look at TikTok. Take a look not at the world that you grew up in but at the world that the next generation is growing up in.

So Barbara and I spent five years deep in Holy of Holies, talking about Eros as Value, about Unique Self, about First Principles and First Values, and about CosmoErotic Humanism—this new Story of Value, which integrated all of the *dharma* thinking that we'd engaged in together, and all the thinking that she and I had each done for the last twenty-five years.

Every time I encountered a *dharma* problem, I tried to solve the problem.

For example, *True Self* thinking was inaccurate and limited, so I tried to solve it by understanding the depths of True Self, but then originated a new understanding called *Unique Self, Evolutionary Unique Self,* and *Unique Self Symphony,* which included and transcended *True Self* to give us a new story of identity.[3]

The new Universe Stories we had were limited, the kind of mythopoetic narrative of people like Mary Evelyn Tucker and Brian Swimme, who were both students of Thomas Berry. Thomas had enormous influence on Brian, who is a mathematical cosmologist and is doing great work. They did this universe story conversation, but it was actually *mythopoetic.* It didn't believe that value was real. It stayed with the standard neo-Darwinian narrative that science has long outstripped.

---

3 See Marc Gafni, *Your Unique Self: The Radical Path to Personal Enlightenment* (Integral, 2012).

It didn't talk about a Field of Eros.[4]

It didn't talk about First Principles and First Values.[5]

It wanted to stay within the postmodern context and *mythopoetically* talk about a better world. I realized that and stepped in to say, "Let's articulate a new Universe Story."

OUTRAGEOUS LOVE AND UNIQUE SELF ARE EVOLUTIONARY EMERGENTS

We stepped deep into creating a new Universe Story. It's not a Kisa Gotami story (about a woman who asked the Buddha how to continue after unbearable tragedy), which is about cultivating compassion. No, it's an Outrageous Love story—and although I cited Tagore and Dante, we are actually talking about something new, a unique emergent called *Outrageous Love*. **This Outrageous Love—Eros—is the very core of Reality. It is throbbing, and it includes sexuality and desire.**

It is something beyond what Dante was talking about, although he had glimmerings of it. It is definitely beyond what the Buddhist stories were talking about, although we include something from the Buddhist stories.

But that's not what it is. It's something new.

Yes, on the one hand, we want to locate it in this very large lineage, including all of the premodern, modern, and postmodern versions. But on the other hand, we are creating something that needs to be created, and that's actually startlingly new. It is an evolutionary emergent.

Ken Wilber and I had a long talk about the Unique Self. We were looking for earlier sources for the Unique Self in the great traditions, whether in

---

4   See Marc Gafni and Kristina Kincaid, *A Return to Eros: The Radical Experience of Being Fully Alive* (BenBella, 2017).

5   See David J. Temple, *First Values and First Principles: Forty-two Propositions on CosmoErotic Humanism, the Meta-crisis, and the World to Come* (World Philosophy and Religion, 2024).

the Ten Ox-Herding Pictures in Buddhism or *Sahaj Samadhi* in Kashmir Shaivism. That's all true—*and* the new story is radically evolving. It is a radically new evolutionary emergent.

This brings us to the question of teacher-student. I want to talk about that, but first, I want to set the context by asking our three fundamental questions: *Who are we? Where are we? What are we doing?*

1. We're *aware* that we're in a time between stories and time between worlds.
2. We want to *do something* about it. In order to actually shift, change, reconfigure, and evolve our world so that it doesn't collapse in the meta-crisis, *we have to evolve the source code.*

The collapse would mean:

- Billions of lives lost in the present.
- Trillions of unborn babies lost in the future.
- All the projects begun in the past remain unfinished.

It will first hit the most disadvantaged among us—not those of us living in comfortable homes in middle-class or upper-class environments. The first two billion people to die and suffer are likely going to die in heat waves in India, which are increasingly likely. Two million people could die in two weeks!

That's what we are doing here: we are trying to avoid the suffering of billions and bring as many human beings (as well as other beings beyond the human) into the circle of Eros, into the circle of Love.

We have to evolve the source code. **We have to change not just the infrastructure of Reality, not just the social structure and governance structures, but the basic story in which we live.** We call it the superstructure, but there are many names for it.

We have to change culture itself by evolving the deep source code.

We can't just *claim* new paradigms and declare them. We have to work so hard and go into the source code itself: we integrate the best of the religious traditions into a new grammar, and integrate the best of systems theory, chaos theory, complexity theory, and all of the emergent sciences.

We need *all* of the insights from across *all* of the fields: from across mathematics, chemistry, molecular biology, sociology, and the eleven or twelve fields of psychology.

We need to integrate it into a story:

- That you can tell to a group of sixty truckers any place in the world,
- That I can tell to an eight-year-old,
- That can actually pass muster at the most sophisticated and evolved Jesuit Academy.

A story that includes and transcends the best wisdom and science but is also an emergent and evolving story.

We can't hide. We have to be courageous. We have to *claim* the emergent. We can't just hide it. Unique Self, as hosted in the Unique Self Institute, is a major emergent.

It's the best tool we have to understand who we are that merges all the theories of identity of Eastern and Western enlightenment in a new synergy.

THE ROOT CAUSE OF EXISTENTIAL RISK IS A GLOBAL INTIMACY DISORDER

When Barbara and I were doing those five years in Holy of Holies, we said that it was not enough to say there are win/lose metrics and that we need social synergy to respond to them, although those are both enormously important.

That's a great start. That was Barbara's start, and Daniel has articulated and picked up pieces of that when he talks about the generator functions of existential risk. But it's deeper than that.

Daniel and I had many talks about this back in 2014, and Barbara and I talked about this incessantly between 2014 and when she passed in 2019: **there is a deeper root cause to these generator functions of existential risk.**

The deeper root cause is a global intimacy disorder.

I know it can get garbled for people, and I can feel the garble, and I want to clarify this.

You've got these two generator functions:

1. Win/lose metrics. Rivalrous conflict governed by win/lose metrics.
2. This generates fragile, complicated systems, and things break down.

We need to move towards what Barbara called "social synergy"—but you can't move towards social synergy unless there is *intimacy*, which is why we said the underlying root cause underneath these generative functions is a global intimacy disorder.

Again, I can feel different people hearing it, even people who have known me for ten years—they think they know those words, and then they stop thinking. Then there's a tired repetition around the way we even repeat it to ourselves.

However, **it has to be completely fresh, completely new each time you say it**. You, we, as the revolution together—we have to re-understand it, re-engage it every day. That's why feminism did consciousness-raising groups. That's why deep changes in society were being talked about in the cafés of Paris (and around the world). If you're not talking about it at a café, if you're not thinking about it when you go to sleep, if it's not causing a conflict between you and your beloveds, then it's not real.

We have to actually *feel* this; we have to actually *find* it.

What do we mean when we say there is a global intimacy disorder underneath?

First, if we are in win/lose metrics, you can't have intimacy because I've reduced you to an "it." You *serve* me. You are *instrumental* to me. You may even be my partner, but you are still instrumental. We cannot really be intimate with each other.

Now, to know what that means, we need to know what intimacy means: **Intimacy is shared identity in the context of (relative) otherness, with mutuality of recognition, mutuality of feeling (pathos), mutuality of purpose (telos), and mutuality of value.**

But if we are stuck in win/lose metrics, there can be no shared identity whatsoever.

Second, win/lose metrics creates the opposite of synergy. Synergy is separate parts creating larger wholes. That means the creation of new intimacies.

Synergy is just another word for intimacy.

But you can use social synergy your whole life and not get it. When Barbara and I first started talking about intimacy, Barbara's like, "Why are we talking about intimacy?" We did this very deep, beautiful dive together. We impacted each other greatly and had a gorgeous ride. One of the things that gradually became clear was that synergy is just another word for intimacy. Synergy means separate parts coming together into a new whole, which has a shared identity in the context of otherness. That's what synergy means.

Complicated systems are systems in which the parts don't know each other; therefore, they are fragile. The supply lines are not connected to their end customers. For example, each country, company, and vector in the international market is vying for its own success, but there is no sense of a larger whole and the *telos* of a larger whole. We don't realize the larger whole has a direction. In a complicated system:

- ◆ I don't participate in a larger whole.
- ◆ I don't try to align myself with the plotline of the larger whole.
- ◆ I pull only for my limited success.
- ◆ I'm a short-termer.
- ◆ I can't see future generations.
- ◆ I'm stuck in the myopic tyranny of the superficial present.

The myopic tyranny of the superficial present creates fragile systems that optimize for efficiency rather than resilience, for windfall profits rather than thriving. And then you leave billions of people out of the safety net. You create polarization, which becomes one of the major vectors of existential risk.

So there is a root cause: a global intimacy disorder. In order to make that real, we need to understand what intimacy is, so we defined intimacy.

But then we need to understand that intimacy, Eros, and uniqueness **are all *values* of Cosmos**. These are First Principles and First Values. These are the mathematics of intimacy of Cosmos. Unless we have a shared Story of Value, we cannot be intimate with each other. It simply can't be done.

When we find that rare moment in life, we find some new person close to us, we realize: Wow, we have a shared Field of Value. It's not just shared *values*. We are in the *Field of Value* together.

If we are not in the Field of Value together, we can't be intimate. **We realized that the global intimacy disorder is rooted in a breakdown of the Field of Value**, in the sense that we've stepped out of the Field of Value.

These are hard-won insights, and we have to get it again and again, so it doesn't become jargon. It's deep.

TEACHING AS LOVEMAKING

Now, within that context, what is the teacher-student relationship?

In this recapitulation we just did, I wasn't *teaching* this. I was just *evoking* it.

In other words, I was assuming that we've talked about this for a decade, but we have to evoke it again and put the pieces together. I wasn't presenting it in a way that I would to someone who had never heard this, but I was trying to evoke its depth.

But to *evoke its depth* is different from *repeating*. And I want to say this tenderly, but even some of the people closest to me start *repeating*. You can't repeat! Don't repeat! Go and learn it, and *know it again*!

That's what we have to do in love. We have to fall in love *again* every day. We have to fall in love with each other.

We have to fall in love with the *dharma*.

We have to fall in love with First Principles and First Values.

We have to fall in love with the distinctions anew, again, originally, every day. Life goes insipid, flaccid, non-erotic, and non-intimate; life becomes desiccated, dry, and inert, when we *repeat*. It doesn't matter whether I am repeating "I love you" or "I think I've heard that before."

I am going to tell you one of the gifts that a student gives a teacher. Let me give you just something from a teacher's perspective.

What is a great student?

A great student listens in a way that they are not thinking, "I got that. I know that. You've said that." If they do, then they never grow. And then, literally in my interior, I go limp. I lose my access to the center. It doesn't matter whether the student is ninety years old or eight years old—that's not the point; it's about someone who is *receiving*—**but in the nature of the receiving, you are *loved open*.** The exchange of teacher and student is always making love. It has nothing to do with sexuality, but it's always *lovemaking*. That's how it's described by the lineage. It's always *zivug*.

What the student has the capacity to do is to receive so deeply that the teacher gets loved open (and in making love, the receiver is always fully active)—and that allows the teacher to enter so deeply that the student gets loved open.

That's what I meant when I said, "The teacher becomes the student; the student becomes the teacher."

In the classical model, the teacher is *dukra*; the teacher is *penetrating*. And the student is *nukva*; the student is *receiving*. That's the classical model. That's a lot by itself. It understands teaching not as sharing of information but as this great act of cosmic Eros performed in the space of mind and heart. **Teaching is cosmic Eros performed in the space of mind, heart, and the transmission.**

The teacher tries to stand in the Field of Value—in *the Tao*.

The teacher tries to *embody* the Field of Value—the intrinsic, inherent (i.e., not socially constructed) *telos* of Reality.

The teacher, if they are real, should have genuine attainment in the Field of Value—even as they are imperfect, flawed, subject to making mistakes, and thus are able to receive feedback.

You should feel them standing in the forever Field, in the Field of Value. You want to know that the teacher is willing to die for Truth, to die for Goodness, to die for Value. You want the teacher not to be making up their own "take on Reality." **You want the teacher to be actually *receiving* in the Field of Eros, in the Field of She, in the Field of the Intimate Universe, and then trying to discern distinction in that Field and then to penetrate the student with those distinctions.**

180

The teacher is fully active, and the student is fully receiving, but then it switches.

How does it switch?

It switches because **in the nature of the student's receiving, they actually penetrate the teacher**. There is this dramatic penetration, which then loves the teacher open, then the teacher opens into the wider field in an entirely different way.

Let me give you an example.

I had a teacher who passed away, and I had nothing to do with him for forty years because I left the classical system of orthodoxy that he taught. But I used to listen to literally *every word* he said, and then I would review every word he said, then I would review it again, and again, and again.

And each time he talked about the same thing, I would be more ecstatic than I was the time before—because I could learn, from the way he said it again, some new nuance.

Even after I left the system that he taught, I tracked everything he did and said because I knew that he was in the Field of Value, and listened to him again, and again, and again, and again—because I wanted to hear everything.

I didn't say, "Okay, I've got this. I've got what he said." No, no, I opened myself up again, and again, and again. During the time when I knew him, he would always be excited to share something with me. In the way that I listened to him, I was receiving it so deeply that he would, in some sense, know it better because he realized that, in some sense, I was penetrating him with my receiving.

It is not listening in a way where there is this kind of subtle egoic structure at play. You can literally feel that. Sometimes I'll talk to someone who I love madly, but their egoic structure is so at play that even though they don't realize it, they just stop listening. And then I go dry. I can't feel it. I can't feel the Eros. I can't feel the Field.

There is this exchange where the teacher becomes the student, and the student becomes the teacher. That's what happens in lovemaking. It's why the teacher-student relationship is lovemaking.

TEACHER-STUDENT RELATIONSHIPS AND THE UNIQUE SELF

To recap:

- First, both the teacher and student are in the Field of Value.
- Two, the teacher wants to transmit to the student a set of discernments in the Field of Value.

But this is not what happens in most teacher-student relationships.

We have teacher-student relationships, let's say in the university, where the assumption is:

- There is no Field of Value—that's the assumption of the Western liberal academy, of the entire university system around the world, both in closed and open societies. It's wrong, for lots of reasons, and we've talked about how we need to re-vision the Field of Value in *First Principles and First Values*.[6]
- The teacher is, at best, transmitting *bits of information*. The teacher's job is to transmit a body of unique information to the student. That's one form. In that sense, there is actually no hierarchy at all between teacher and student. The teacher happens to have a piece of information, and they give it to the student.

---

6   See David J. Temple, *First Values and First Principles: Forty-two Propositions on CosmoErotic Humanism, the Meta-crisis, and the World to Come* (World Philosophy and Religion, 2024).

That's one form of teacher-student relationship. It's legitimate, and those relationships should happen. That form should exist, but that's not what we are talking about. It uses the term *teacher-student*, but it's talking about something entirely different.

The second possibility, which is the more classic form in the East, is that the teacher has this deep attainment of *enlightenment*, but enlightenment is usually not identified properly with *Value*. It is enlightenment in this deep sense of the Field of Oneness, which tells the person what their true identity is: I am not just separate; I am part of the Field of Oneness, which is true, good, and beautiful.

That's great, and the teacher has *more* of that realization. The teacher is, in some sense, more enlightened. They are claiming they have more attainment of enlightenment (as they may well do). They try to share that experience of enlightenment with the student. The teacher has more enlightenment or more what we call in the formal language, *True Self*. My True Self is that I'm part of the One, part of the singular that has no plural.

The teacher has more True Self, so they say: "Because I have more True Self, I also have *authority* over you. The teacher begins to assume authority over the student." Now, authority *per se* is not bad, but if the teacher assumes authority over dimensions where the teacher should have no authority, it collapses.

Overall, this doesn't work because the student is not *just* oneness or consciousness, the student is a *unique expression* of consciousness. The teacher can't have more uniqueness than the student has—if I realize that I am not just *True* Self, but I am actually *Unique* Self, which is not just the talents and skills of the separate self.

- Level one, separate self: skin-encapsulated ego.
- Level two: I'm not just separate. I'm part of the one True Self.
- Level three, Unique Self: I am a unique expression of the Field, which is seamless but not featureless.

By the way, *seamless but not featureless* is not a quote from Whitehead but a unique way that we say things in CosmoErotic Humanism. I originally read a version of this in a several-volume epic by a guy named R.H. Blyth, called *Zen and Zen Classics*. That's where this phrase came from, but we are doing something new and original with it. We are using it in a particular way.

In his *Zen Classics* book, he was using it in a very different way, but not unrelated, which is why I brought it to bear. But we are using it in a new emergent way:

The Unique Self is seamless but not featureless. Unique Self means: **I am a unique expression of this Field, but this Field is not just this Field of Consciousness—it's a Field of Value, a Field of ErosValue. It's a Field of ErosDesire, Intimacy, and Value, and I'm a unique expression of that Field.**

If that quality exists in a human being, then it's unique in the person, so the teacher can have no authority over that.

The teacher is still transmitting to the student. There is still a natural, appropriate, holistic hierarchy of attainment in which the teacher is sharing. There is:

- A full egalitarianism in terms of power, as everyone has their own individuated autonomy.
- The transmission from the teacher, this sense in which the teacher is what's called the *dukra*, an active penetrating force, and the student is the *nukva*, a receptive force.

AUTONOMY AND COMMUNION IN TEACHER-STUDENT RELATIONSHIP

Then there are moments when the student may have some original insight that they share with the teacher, and in that moment, the student actually becomes the teacher, which is beautiful, but not because they just made something up.

It's one of the conversations Barbara and I always had. Barbara would say to everyone, "Oh, that's your *dharma*, that's beautiful," but she didn't really mean it. It was a way of just facilitating people. And Barbara and I really got to this deep understanding, "No, no, you can't just *say* something. You can't just *claim* something."

You have to fully receive, fully honor, and appropriately cite, the places where you received pieces, a sentence here, and a sentence here, and a sentence here. The text is: **anyone who says something in the name of the person who said it brings redemption to the world**.

It's not just that *it's all flowing through us*. There are also unique places where we receive this very deep, broad, real, and beautiful *original penetration*. I've got to receive that. Then, once I've received that, then I might have something new to say, or I might have the same thing to say, but I'll say it with a unique quality of intimacy. I might have something new to add to it, or I might say it just through my being in a way that's so special, beautiful, and original.

I'll just give you an example. Yesterday, I was doing a Holy of Holies with Ted, and he shared with me a podcast that he did, in which he was literally saying the *dharma*. I actually heard him say the *dharma*. He wasn't *adding* to it, but it was also completely original and fresh. And I was super proud of him. It was original and fresh because it was going through *Ted-ness*. I could feel an expansion of the *dharma* through *Ted-ness* that couldn't happen through anyone else because he had actually put his egoic self aside. By putting his egoic self aside, he then emerged in his full uniqueness of presence.

It's a very subtle thing. It all happens here in this place. **The teacher-student relationship is this place in which we are in this Field of ErosValue together.** It's beautiful.

- We are in this Field of Eros Value together.
- We are all equal in the Field. We all have a unique expression of the Field. There is full egalitarianism in terms of everybody's fundamental Value.
- We all have different roles to play in the Field. In this incarnation, there are teachers and students, and in a different incarnation, that might change. But in this incarnation, there is a distinct teacher-student relationship.

If I take someone as a teacher, I've got to go *all the way* with that—not to give them authority over me in places where it's inappropriate, not to give them any authority over me in terms of the decisions I make in my life—and yet I fully receive in order to be *impacted*.

We *should* be impacted. We are not just autonomous. We are also communion—intimate communion. And when we're in the Field of Value together, looking at a shared horizon, we must listen to each other.

A teacher should have an impact on a student—*and* a student should have ultimate autonomy and ultimate power. The teacher should always bow to that power, always bow to that autonomy, and always bow to the independent integrity of the student's decision-making. That should always be true.

Teachers should never arrogate any power over the decision-making of a student. Ultimately, the student always has to choose.

A teacher should be in radical devotion to the student. **The teacher and student should be in radical devotion to each other, and they should be in devotion together to the Field of *She*, to the Field of Value.**

And there is *transmission*, which is real. There is *penetration*, and then there is *mutual* penetration—we love each other open. It's this very deep and subtle play. Enormous possibility opens up in the teacher-student relationship.

FROM THE CONVENTIONAL TO THE POST-CONVENTIONAL

I want to make it really clear: the depth of teacher-student relationship that I'm describing is not for everybody. What I just described was not a 101 course, but the advanced course.

What I described is not what I would suggest as the model for every situation, but that's what is possible. I'm not suggesting this is what should happen every place, everywhere. I'm not suggesting that at all.

In general, for most people, most of the time, very clear delineations work.

We should circumscribe teachers.

We should empower students.

We should probably not have dual relationships and not have blurred roles, et cetera.

That's all generally true—for most people, most of the time. And then sometimes we get to a place where that's not enough. As we move from the conventional to what Kohlberg calls the "post-conventional," new possibilities begin to open up.

I'm not suggesting this for everyone.

This is for a particular developmental structure of consciousness, for people who want to take their unique risk in Eros and Love, and actually become part of a Unique Self Symphony, and speak into the meta-crisis, live into the meta-crisis.

It's not a hobby.

It's not: *I am trying to establish myself and paper over my emptiness, my frustration, my anxiety, my rage, and my anger at all the times of my life by propping myself up in some egoic way in the world.*

If that's what you're doing, this is the wrong place. And of course, everyone is doing that a little bit—we are all holy and broken *Hallelujahs*. That's okay. But there's got to be something much more powerful and much deeper at play.

What we tried to do now is to move into the source code, to find each other and establish the field together.

I hope everybody felt, or at least most people, that I wasn't talking *at* you. I was just trying to feel *with* you and find my way with you.

The depth of "thee" creates "me," which creates "we," and then we create each other, and we find each other in the symphony. It happens on so many levels.

So thank you.

Thank you. Thank you. Thank you.

INDEX

VOLUME 19

LIST OF EPISODES